THE BEDFORD SERIES IN HISTORY AND CULTURE

Selections from
The Cotton Kingdom

by Frederick Law Olmsted

Related Titles in
THE BEDFORD SERIES IN HISTORY AND CULTURE
Advisory Editors: Lynn Hunt, *University of California, Los Angeles*
David W. Blight, *Yale University*
Bonnie G. Smith, *Rutgers University*
Natalie Zemon Davis, *University of Toronto*

THE BEDFORD SERIES IN HISTORY AND CULTURE

Selections from
The Cotton Kingdom
by Frederick Law Olmsted

Abridged with an Introduction by

John C. Inscoe
University of Georgia

BEDFORD / ST. MARTIN'S   Boston ◆ New York

For Bedford / St. Martin's

Senior Executive Editor for History and Technology: William J. Lombardo
Director of Development for History: Jane Knetzger
Assistant Production Editor: Lidia MacDonald-Carr
Senior Production Supervisor: Lisa McDowell
Executive Marketing Manager: Sandra McGuire
Project Management: Books By Design, Inc.
Cartography: Mapping Specialists, Ltd.
Senior Art Director: Anna Palchik
Text Design: Claire Seng-Niemoeller
Cover Design: William Boardman
Cover Art: From Frederick Law Olmsted, *A Journey in the Seaboard Slave States; With Remarks on Their Economy* (London: Sampson Low, Son, & Co.; New York: Dix and Edwards, 1856), p. 387.
Composition: Achorn International, Inc.
Printing and Binding: RR Donnelley and Sons

Manufactured in the United States of America.

9 8 7 6 5 4
f e d c b a

For information, write: Bedford / St. Martin's, 75 Arlington Street, Boston, MA 02116 (617-399-4000)

ISBN 978-1-4576-0713-4

Acknowledgments

Main document: From Arthur M. Schlesinger, ed., *The Cotton Kingdom: A Traveller's Observations on Cotton & Slavery in the American Slave States*, by Frederick Law Olmsted (New York: Alfred A. Knopf, 1953).

Acknowledgments and copyrights appear on the same page as the text and art selections they cover; these acknowledgments and copyrights constitute an extension of the copyright page. It is a violation of the law to reproduce these selections by any means whatsoever without the written permission of the copyright holder.

About the cover: This illustration, from Frederick Law Olmsted's 1856 book, *A Journey in the Seaboard Slave States; With Remarks on Their Economy*, depicts slaves, both male and female, completing road repairs near a plantation in South Carolina.

Foreword

The Bedford Series in History and Culture is designed so that readers can study the past as historians do.

The historian's first task is finding the evidence. Documents, letters, memoirs, interviews, pictures, movies, novels, or poems can provide facts and clues. Then the historian questions and compares the sources. There is more to do than in a courtroom, for hearsay evidence is welcome, and the historian is usually looking for answers beyond act and motive. Different views of an event may be as important as a single verdict. How a story is told may yield as much information as what it says.

Along the way the historian seeks help from other historians and perhaps from specialists in other disciplines. Finally, it is time to write, to decide on an interpretation and how to arrange the evidence for readers.

Each book in this series contains an important historical document or group of documents, each document a witness from the past and open to interpretation in different ways. The documents are combined with some element of historical narrative—an introduction or a biographical essay, for example—that provides students with an analysis of the primary source material and important background information about the world in which it was produced.

Each book in the series focuses on a specific topic within a specific historical period. Each provides a basis for lively thought and discussion about several aspects of the topic and the historian's role. Each is short enough (and inexpensive enough) to be a reasonable one-week assignment in a college course. Whether as classroom or personal reading, each book in the series provides firsthand experience of the challenge—and fun—of discovering, recreating, and interpreting the past.

Lynn Hunt
David W. Blight
Bonnie G. Smith
Natalie Zemon Davis

Preface

Outside observers have provided among the richest primary sources for scholars of the antebellum South. Despite the stereotypical assumptions, florid prose, and regional and moral biases that characterized the majority of such travel accounts by northerners and foreigners, their detailed descriptions of the people and places encountered have often been of great value to modern historians of slavery and other aspects of southern society as it existed in the decades before the Civil War.

Probably the most valuable of such accounts are the writings produced by a journalist from Connecticut, Frederick Law Olmsted, in the 1850s and early 1860s. Olmsted published three lengthy books of description and commentary based on fourteen months of travel through the South from 1852 to 1854 as a correspondent for the *New York Daily Times*. In 1861, Olmsted condensed the three books into a single work, *The Cotton Kingdom*. Although it was his later career as a landscape architect, environmentalist, and urban planner for which Olmsted is most widely remembered, this much briefer stint as a correspondent and social critic was an equally significant part of his legacy, especially to historians.

Because his self-described mission to observe and report objectively on slavery and its effects on southern society was so thorough and precise, his route so extensive, and his observations so wide-ranging and insightful, Olmsted's work remains the most cited and quoted of any contemporary source on the "peculiar institution." He provided astute assessments of nearly every aspect of southern life—class structure as well as racial distinctions; urban life as well as plantation and small farm life; and a host of economic enterprises, both agricultural and industrial. Olmsted covered more territory than any other antebellum traveler. Over the course of a little more than a year and a half and on two different trips, he moved down the Atlantic seaboard, across the Deep South and up the lower Mississippi Valley, westward through much of

Texas, before heading back east through the "interior cotton districts," and finally into the Appalachian highlands, which he labeled the "back country."

The Cotton Kingdom originally appeared as two volumes and consisted of a total of 780 pages. In selecting passages for inclusion in this much-abbreviated version, I have sought to convey the full range of locales, experiences, and attitudes that Olmsted encountered and described so vividly. I have also tried to include what are among the most revealing features of his narratives — his many interviews with a vast range of individuals, including white and black, rich and poor, urban and rural, educated and noneducated, and people from all sections of the South. The cumulative effect of this sampler is a representative sense of the many variables and complexities of this fully entrenched system of human bondage in terms of its functions and labor demands; its economic strengths and weaknesses; and the contrasting lifestyles of slaveholders, nonslaveholders, and slaves, and what members of all three groups thought about the institution that so indelibly defined their society and their lives.

The introduction provides a biographical overview of Olmsted's life, particularly his formative years and the circumstances that led him to undertake his southern mission when he did. It also seeks to make sense of the volatile political climate in which Olmsted carried out that assignment and the escalation of sectional tensions that made his observations so relevant and timely to readers on both sides of the Atlantic. A chronology serves to reinforce the interplay of these developments, both personal and political, while a select bibliography provides a sampler of the extensive biographical treatments of Olmsted himself, as well as key works of recent scholarship on those issues with which he wrestled in *The Cotton Kingdom*, and on the crisis that proved so integral to its production.

A NOTE ON THE TEXT

The text that follows all comes from Olmsted's *The Cotton Kingdom*. Both the chapter divisions and subsections have been imposed by the editor and do not reflect the arrangement of the book as organized by Olmsted, though the order in which the text appears reflects that of the original and maintains the sequential order of his travels.

ACKNOWLEDGMENTS

I am grateful to Katherine Rohrer, a Ph.D. student at the University of Georgia, who has made good use of Olmsted's writings in her own work on southern women and slavery, for her help copying and organizing the materials used in this volume. I have also benefited from discussions with and feedback from good friends and former students of mine, George Justice and Christopher Lawton, both of whom have focused on antebellum Georgia, have considerable experience in teaching the South, and continue to find fresh and innovative ways of utilizing primary source materials in their courses.

I have found Olmsted's work of much value in my own early work on slavery in Southern Appalachia, and I appreciate the opportunities I've had to publish my own thoughts about his travels in that region in particular, thanks to editors such as Dwight Billings, James Klotter, and the editors of the journal *Slavery & Abolition*.

I appreciate the good guidance and patience of Bedford/St. Martin's editor William Lombardo as I first moved into and through this process. I am grateful to executive editor Elizabeth Welch for the superb first-round of editing of both my work and Olmsted's, and for the subsequent rounds of equally good care and attention to our work by Laura Kintz, Nancy Benjamin, and Lidia MacDonald-Carr.

I would also like to thank the reviewers whose comments helped shape the book's introduction and abridgement: Gary Edwards, Arkansas State University; Mark Elliott, University of North Carolina at Greensboro; Matthew Mason, Brigham Young University; and John Mayfield, Samford University.

John C. Inscoe

Contents

Illustrations

Selections from
The Cotton Kingdom

by Frederick Law Olmsted

PART ONE

Introduction: A Connecticut Yankee in King Cotton's Court

When Frederick Law Olmsted crossed the Mason-Dixon Line on his first venture into the American South in December 1852, he carried with him a thirty-year lifetime of experiences. Yet it was far more than his personal past, as varied in experience as that was, that shaped his mission and the publications that resulted from it. Olmsted became, at that moment, part of a long and still expanding tradition of southern commentary and travel writing by outside observers. More often than not, slavery was a central focus of those visitors who felt compelled to chronicle their impressions of the region in print.

Olmsted's three trips to the South, during which he spent a total of fourteen months in ten states between late 1852 and mid-1854, took place in the midst of a decade of increased sectional strife—rampant abolitionist activity, territorial and legal controversies, and political partisanship that would, by decade's end, reach a breaking point between North and South. The published work that resulted from his travels both fueled and was fueled by these developments. It appeared first as newspaper columns in 1853 and 1854, then in book form between 1856 and 1860—three volumes that totaled nearly two thousand pages of text.[1] Only in the fall of 1861, after the Civil War had broken out, did a compilation of that work appear in print. Published first in England under the title *The Cotton Kingdom*, that condensation of the three earlier works reflects the evolution of Olmsted's views over the course of the nine years since he began his southern ventures. At the beginning, he touted his objectivity and lack of bias in terms of the morality of

1

southern slaveholding. By 1861, the nation was at war, and any pretense of neutrality in Olmsted's attitude toward the South had disappeared. Although it is his later career as a landscape architect, environmentalist, and urban planner for which Olmsted is most widely remembered, his much briefer stint as a correspondent and social critic is an equally significant part of his legacy. *The Cotton Kingdom*, of all his writings, had the greatest impact at the time and, for historians, has had the most lasting value since.

EYEWITNESSES TO SOUTHERN SLAVERY

Antebellum Americans outside the South came to understand slavery as it existed below the Mason-Dixon Line (between Maryland and Pennsylvania) in a variety of ways and from a variety of sources.[2] Fugitive slave narratives were among the most compelling of these sources, if only because they conveyed so intimately and with such immediacy the personal traumas of those who had triumphed over the oppression—both physical and psychological—they had endured as bondsmen and bondswomen. As speakers and as writers (often in collaboration with abolitionist sponsors and colleagues), Frederick Douglass, Solomon Northup, Josiah Henson, Henry Bibb, William Wells Brown, Harriet Jacobs, and William and Ellen Craft, along with many others, told and retold the stories of their lives as slaves and their often dramatic escapes north to audiences and readerships that grew more enthralled and more incensed as the abolitionist movement intensified in the 1850s.[3]

Another form of firsthand testimony also proved to be effective antislavery propaganda—that of several whites who had lived on southern plantations and were troubled by what they observed of the lives and labor of their families' black workforces. The most prominent of these were two sisters. Sarah and Angelina Grimké were born and raised in a planter family in Charleston, South Carolina, before moving to Philadelphia, where they became Quakers and soon thereafter emerged as outspoken advocates of abolitionism and women's suffrage. The British actress Fanny Kemble, who spent ten months on the Georgia rice and cotton plantations of her new husband, Pierce Butler, wrote a scathing chronicle of the conditions suffered by his slaves there. Levi Coffin grew up in a Quaker family in North Carolina and moved with them to Indiana as an adult. He became a leader of the Underground Railroad movement and wrote about the traumas of the slave trade as he had observed it in childhood and of his dealings with fugitive slaves.[4]

Other abolitionists witnessed the horrors of the "peculiar institution"—a southern euphemism for slavery—only from the peripheries. William Lloyd Garrison's ventures below the Mason-Dixon Line were limited to trips to Baltimore; Benjamin Lundy lived for several years in Wheeling, Virginia (later West Virginia); and before she wrote *Uncle Tom's Cabin* (1852), Harriet Beecher Stowe made only one trip to Kentucky and drew her impressions of slavery primarily from the vantage point of her home across the Ohio River in Cincinnati, the northern entry point for many escaped slaves.[5] Though they lacked firsthand experience, all these individuals wrote vividly about the cruel treatment of slaves by their masters, families split at slave markets and auctions, and men and women locked in chains as traders moved them south.

Northern and foreign travelers who made more extensive forays into the South often contributed significant commentary on slavery. Some went into the region for the express purpose of providing a northern readership with firsthand fodder for their own antislavery agendas, often drawing on slaves' own words to indict the system under which they lived. Aside from Olmsted, no one traveled more extensively through the region or wrote a more scathing exposé of the conditions under which slaves suffered than the British-born abolitionist James Redpath. Like Olmsted, Redpath set out in the mid-1850s as a correspondent for a New York newspaper—Horace Greeley's *Tribune*. Also like Olmsted, Redpath then compiled his dispatches into a book, *The Roving Editor; or, Talks with Slaves in the Southern States* (1859).[6] Two decades earlier, abolitionist Theodore Dwight Weld, Angelina Grimké's husband, had recognized the power of such firsthand testimony in mobilizing antislavery sentiment among northern readers and compiled a remarkable body of both inside and outside observations into a volume he called *American Slavery as It Is*, with an only slightly exaggerated subtitle, *Testimony of a Thousand Witnesses*.[7]

Other northerners, in the South for different reasons, were so shocked or troubled by what they saw that the experience itself made them converts to abolitionism and inspired them to articulate their reactions in print. "No man can visit the South for the first time without having his views of slavery, whatever they may be, to some extent modified," declared Charles Grandison Parson, a Boston physician, in his book, *An Inside View of Slavery*, which he published in 1855 upon his return from a tour of Georgia and adjacent states.[8] Foreign visitors to the United States, especially in the 1830s and 1840s, included the South as part of their "grand tour," and many of them—Karl Bernhard of Germany, Frederika Bremer of Sweden, and numerous English men

Frederick Law Olmsted, ca. 1860
Associated Press.

and women, such as Sir Charles Lyell, Harriet Martineau, and James Silk Buckingham—commented on slavery and southern life in lengthy travel narratives aimed at enlightening European readers on American life, north and south. While clearly critical of the system and the poor treatment of slaves, their observations were often no more than anecdotal and incidental, and never as integral to their travel accounts as those with more fully defined abolitionist agendas.[9]

Of all these varied accounts—oral and written, fictional and nonfictional, in newspapers, pamphlets, journals, and books—none came from an observer of the antebellum South who traveled more extensively through it or wrote more thoroughly or more systematically about it than Frederick Law Olmsted, a Connecticut native turned New York journalist, who set out in the winter of 1852 with an assignment to do just that.

OLMSTED'S FORMATIVE YEARS

Much in Frederick Law Olmsted's early life contributed to the circumstances and the outcome of his ventures into the South. Born in Hartford, Connecticut, in 1822, he was the first of two sons of a moderately successful owner of a dry goods store. Olmsted's mother died when he was just three years old, and his father quickly remarried. Both his father and stepmother enjoyed traveling, and they allowed their two boys, Fred (as he was called) and his younger brother, John Hull, to roam freely. Fred noted in later autobiographical writings that he took pleasure in "conditions of scenery" from an early age and that "while I was but a half grown lad, my parents thought well to let me wander as few parents are willing their children should."[10] Among Olmsted's most vivid memories of childhood were traveling with his family through the Connecticut Valley and beyond, which infused in him a wanderlust that remained integral to his life and various careers. "I had before I was twelve," he recalled in later years, "traveled much with my father and mother by stage coach, canal, and steamboat, visiting West Point, Trenton Falls, Niagara, Quebec, Lake George."[11]

Olmsted's schooling evoked less fond memories, consisting of sporadic stints in grammar schools, "dame schools" (private elementary schools usually taught by women), occasional homeschooling, and tutelage by an array of clergymen, to whom he was farmed out as part of a relentless quest by his father to find the proper mentor for his eldest son. Given the irregularity of his formal education, Olmsted credited extensive reading on his own to his strong command of geography, politics, and the natural sciences, which would serve him so well as a young adult. At the age of fifteen, he was set to enroll at Yale University but had to give up the opportunity due to an eye infection caused by the poisonous sumac plant. He would visit his brother, John, there on a number of occasions, but his own higher education consisted of a lengthy internship under an eminent civil engineer and a brief teaching stint at Phillips Academy in Andover, Massachusetts.[12]

Neither of those ventures led to solid career paths for Olmsted, and in 1842 his father sent him to clerk with a fellow dry goods merchant in New York City, where he remained for a year and a half. At that point, discontented with his father's profession, he yielded to the impulse to travel, and in 1843 he signed aboard a ship sailing to China, with the lowly rank of apprentice seaman. One of his biographers noted, "In his unsettled state, eager for knowledge of a larger world of adventure, he turned to the sea—the ultimate symbol of romantic yearning—and to the adventure that has beckoned many Americans seeking to find the meeting of mind and body."[13] The yearlong voyage was a searing experience: on top of rough seas and weather, a tyrannical captain made life miserable for the crew, and too-brief stays in port and his own ill health kept Olmsted from observing much of Asian life, which had been a large impetus for making the trip. Much later, he took the opportunity to write about the experience in a lengthy published essay called "A Voice from the Sea," a harsh critique of all the problems he had endured and a call for reform in commanders' treatment of their sailors.[14]

Shifting gears once again, Olmsted took an interest in farming and scientific agriculture, spurred in part by sitting in on lectures while visiting his brother at Yale. After apprenticeships on small farms in Connecticut and New York, he convinced his father in 1848 to invest in a 130-acre tract on New York's Staten Island, a once prosperous farm that had deteriorated, and set himself to restoring its productivity by applying modern methods and theories. While he was only partially successful, the experience proved a rewarding one for Fred, as he mobilized neighboring farmers to adopt "model farm" practices to improve their own output and exchange ideas through a county agricultural society. While farming, too, proved a fleeting venture for this young man still in search of a vocation, Olmsted's later travel writings would be enhanced by his observations and commentary on agriculture, which he saw as central to defining the societies he found himself critiquing.

In 1850, a new opportunity to travel abroad presented itself to Olmsted. His brother, John, and John's roommate at Yale, Charles Loring

Brace, were planning a trip through the British Isles and continental Europe, and Olmsted was eager to join them. For six months, the three-some traveled together, often on foot. Olmsted was particularly attuned to British agricultural practices, but he also became enamored of rural landscape, both natural and planned, thus planting the seeds of his future career. Upon his return, he retired to his Staten Island farm and devoted his energies to chronicling the trip. *Walks and Talks of an American Farmer in England* was published in two volumes in 1852, by the New York publisher G. P. Putnam. It established the model of travel writing that would characterize his coverage of the American South in the years ahead. According to one commentator, *Walks and Talks* "proved that he had genuine literary ability, could construct revealing dialogue and authentic regional dialect, knew how to draw out information in interviews, and above all possessed a trained eye for social conditions as well as for the details of farming and landscape."[15]

TARGETING THE SOUTH

By February 1852, when *Walks and Talks* established him as an accomplished travel writer and celebrated "man of letters," it occurred to both Olmsted and his friend Brace that he might make the American South the next means of satisfying his inclinations as a roving reporter. Southern slavery had come into sharp focus for Olmsted during his English tour. He had been struck, indeed stung, by how critical the British were of the institution and how often they raised the topic when talking to Americans like himself. It generated "a hundred times more hard feeling in England toward America" than all other issues, he noted with surprise.[16] Henry J. Raymond, editor of the newly established *New York Daily Times* (later simply the *New York Times*), just happened to be thinking about a series of reports on slavery and the southern economy at the time, and Brace, an acquaintance of Raymond's, was quick to recommend his friend and traveling companion as the ideal correspondent for such an assignment. A meeting of Raymond and Olmsted sealed the deal in October, and the latter began plans for his assignment as a roving reporter, which he was ready to undertake a mere two months later.[17]

The timing for such a venture was opportune. Sectional fervor was intensifying throughout the country. The vast new territory acquired by the United States in 1848 as a result of the Mexican War—the former Mexican provinces of California, New Mexico, and a slightly expanded southern boundary of Texas—brought back into the political arena the issue of slavery's future in the West. The debate over California's status as slave or free came to a head when it sought statehood in 1850, and that action served as the impetus for the makeshift and ultimately fragile Compromise of 1850, cobbled together by Congress to work through the sectional impasse. Especially volatile was the inclusion of the Fugitive Slave Act; many in the North vehemently opposed this congressional mandate to penalize anyone attempting to aid or abet the escape of southern slaves moving north or inhibiting efforts by their owners to reclaim them. At the same time, southerners much resented the fact that the law—the compromise's only genuine concession made to the South—was widely flouted and even overturned by local statutes in many parts of the North.

Abolitionist fervor was fueled even further by the publication of Harriet Beecher Stowe's best-selling novel, *Uncle Tom's Cabin*, in March 1852. Conveying the moral principles of abolitionism in heartrending personal situations, Stowe's melodramatic saga drew new attention to the inhumanity of southern slavery and launched the most widespread and emotion-laden wave of sentiment yet against the so-called peculiar institution, both throughout the northern states and abroad. It was at this point that Olmsted found himself ready to weigh in on this new level of frenzied propagandizing. Both he and Raymond saw this as a timely opportunity to get at the reality behind the sentimental scenario painted by Stowe, which Olmsted himself had read and characterized as part of "the deluge of spoony fancy pictures now at its height."[18] Olmsted's experience as a farmer, as much as his well-received *Walks and Talks*, helped convince Raymond that he had found in Brace's young friend a correspondent experienced enough to take on an assignment of such import for his fledgling, and at that point floundering, newspaper.

Curiously, Raymond failed to ask Olmsted about his personal views on slavery before granting him this assignment. Perhaps he knew already that he had found a northerner far more moderately inclined on the subject than either Stowe or the raised levels of abolitionist rhetoric her novel helped fuel. Olmsted made it clear that he disapproved of slavery and considered the North's economic system, which relied on free labor, vastly superior to the South's, which depended on black bondage. He fully shared northerners' offense at the Fugitive Slave Act, confiding to a friend that he "would take in a fugitive slave & shoot a man that was likely to get him."[19] And yet he did not feel that slavery's existence warranted the ever-harsher indictments of either the South as a region or its slaveholders. He resisted casting blame on those perpetuating the labor system on which they were so dependent and insisted on "looking upon slavery as an unfortunate circumstance, for which the people of the South were in no wise to blame."[20] And neither before, during, nor after his excursions in the South did Olmsted ever convey much sympathy for the plight that slaves themselves were forced to endure.

Despite the fact that his closest friend and confidant, Charles Brace, had long been a strong opponent of slavery and sought to convert him to the cause, Olmsted remained disdainful of what he saw as abolitionist fanaticism, arrogance, and impracticality. He felt that slavery could only be ended gradually and with considerable forethought on the part of white America, both North and South. "I do not see that a mere setting free of the blacks," he wrote, "if it could be accomplished, would remedy these evils," nor did he believe it to be "a matter that could be accomplished by this generation." Nevertheless, he felt that it was inevitable that emancipation would be achieved eventually. He even held out some hope that slaveholders themselves might be part of the solution, noting optimistically that if they "were so disposed, it appears to me that there would be no difficulty whatever, politically, financially, socially, in diminishing the evil of slavery, and in preparing the way for an end to it."[21]

Thus Olmsted insisted that he approached his southern assignment as open-mindedly and objectively as any outsider could. "Few men could have been so little inclined to establish previously formed opinions as I was when I began my journey in the South," he later claimed. He vowed to "consider the subject of slavery in a rational, philosophical, and conciliatory spirit," and he suggested that many of the attacks on it from the North were based on exceptional situations rather than normal circumstances, and as such served as the source of "much mischief." He was determined "to see things for myself, and to see them carefully and fairly."[22] One reason Brace pushed the idea of Olmsted's investigative tour of the South was that he thought that exposure to the reality of slavery might lead Olmsted to embrace a more abolitionist position — to "be shaken out of his gradualist stance," as one biographer put it.[23] Yet Olmsted confided to another friend just prior to his first trip, "I am not a red-hot Abolitionist like Charley [Brace], but am a moderate Free Soiler. . . . On the whole, I guess I represent pretty fairly the average sentiment of good thinking on our side."[24]

TRAVELING THE SOUTH

With his Staten Island farm still a primary concern, Olmsted waited until after the 1852 fall harvest to head south, with plans to be back home by March for spring planting. For almost four months, he would travel by train, steamboat, and stagecoach, and occasionally on horseback and on foot. Along the way, he stayed in city hotels and boardinghouses, country inns, and as a guest at a variety of homes and plantations to which he had letters of introduction or other contacts made through his Yale and New York connections.

Olmsted took a train to Washington, D.C., early in December, and he spent several days visiting nearby farms and plantations in Maryland and northern Virginia, before moving on to Richmond, which he also used as a base from which to visit surrounding rural areas for the rest of the month. In January, he moved east to visit Norfolk and then south to the Great Dismal Swamp, before pushing into eastern North Carolina; he took a steamship from Wilmington to Charleston, South Carolina, where he explored the Low Country for a week. He moved down the coast to Savannah, Georgia, where he explored neighboring counties before heading due west through the Georgia and Alabama "black belt" (prime land for cotton plantations worked by slaves), stopping in Columbus and Montgomery for several days in February. He then moved south—again by boat—to the Gulf Coast, arriving in Mobile, Alabama, in mid-February and traveling on to New Orleans, where he spent the rest of the month. At the beginning of March, he traveled up the Mississippi and Red rivers for several days before returning to New Orleans. He then headed north by steamboat, visiting Vicksburg (curiously, his only stop in Mississippi) and then Memphis, Tennessee, in mid-March before heading east across the upper South by train, arriving back in New York on April 6.[25]

From the start, Olmsted made note of the social structure of the cities and towns he moved through, but he elaborated even more on the agricultural practices and use of slave labor on the tobacco, rice, cotton, and sugar plantations that he made a point of visiting on each leg of his journey—no doubt a reflection of his own proclivities as a farmer. The first of his dispatches back to Henry Raymond appeared in the *New York Daily Times* on February 16, 1853; forty-seven more reports appeared at roughly weekly intervals over the next year as columns titled simply "The South." Olmsted felt he had to maintain anonymity during his southern travels and even after his return home. (He claimed that he could imitate a southern accent well enough that he was never recognized as a northerner, though he would willingly admit his origins if asked directly.) He chose the byline "Yeoman," both to keep his identity a secret and to emphasize the one authoritative claim on which he could rest his commentary: his own experience as a tiller of the soil.

Olmsted split his time between writing and farming through the rest of the spring and summer of 1853. His published dispatches were widely read and generated a generally positive response from northern

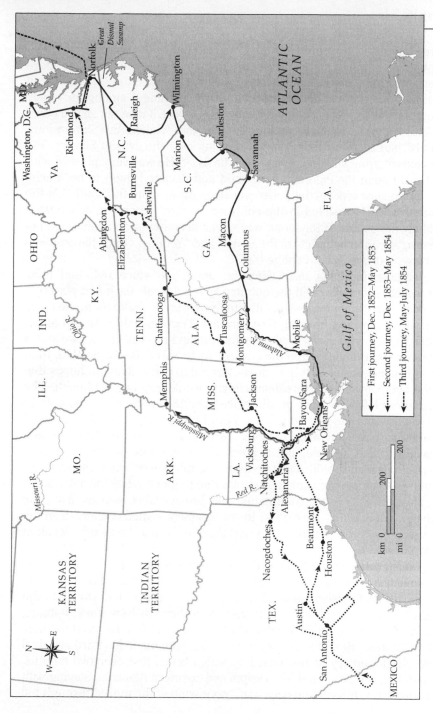

Olmsted's Travels through the American South, 1852–1854

readers. Yet they proved controversial as well, with Olmsted's so-called objectivity drawing fire from both proslavery advocates and the more ardent abolitionists. A Savannah newspaper accused the *Daily Times* of generating unwelcome discord: "It sends a stranger among us 'to spy out the nakedness of the land.' What is its object, if it be not an evil one?" At the other extreme, Raymond reported that "violent Anti-Slavery journals" had accused the paper of "glossing over the evils of Slavery, and discussing the subject upon a false basis."[26] He was very pleased with the attention the columns generated and declared them to be "decidedly the best reports that have ever been made about the South." At the same time, he reveled in the controversy they generated, as Olmsted likely did as well.[27] Raymond was eager to commission a new round of reports from other parts of the South, and "Yeoman," once his crop was harvested, was glad to oblige him.

Interest in Texas and California, states only since 1845 and 1850, respectively, ran high in the country, given the role each had played in the recent war with Mexico. Olmsted proposed to make them the focus of his second trip, moving first through Texas and then on to California, thus providing his readers with firsthand reports on the two states whose status had spurred the current sectional crisis. His brother, John Hull, struggling with tuberculosis, agreed to come along, in hopes that the open air and southwestern climate would improve his health. The brothers left New York in mid-November 1853 and arrived by ship in New Orleans early in December. They immediately headed up the Red River to Natchitoches, Louisiana, where they purchased horses and a mule, hired a guide, and headed across the state border to begin a saddle trip that would span two thousand miles over nearly five months, more often than not camping out. During that time, they toured Texas's cities, towns, rugged mountains, and broad plains, moving from the rapidly developing Gulf coast to the sparsely settled western frontier. At one point, the brothers crossed the Rio Grande to spend a week in Mexico.[28]

Due to reports of Indian trouble farther west, the Olmsteds abandoned their plans to travel to California, and in late May 1854 they returned to Louisiana instead. There the brothers parted ways, as John Hull returned to New Orleans and from there to New York. Fatigue, poor diet, and rough travel conditions seem to have countered the benefits of fresh air and exercise for him, and Fred made his third and final southern journey alone. That leg, which lasted just over two months, took him across central Mississippi and northern Alabama. Staying with various planters and, on occasion, "poor whites," he moved through hill country that eventually led him, by late June, to Chattanooga. For much of July, he traveled, mostly on foot, through the southern Appalachians of Tennessee, North Carolina, and Virginia, a region he would collectively label the "back country." On July 29, he found himself back in Richmond and proceeded by steamboat to New York, where he arrived on August 2, after nearly nine months away from home.[29] Literary critic Edmund Wilson summed up Olmsted's feat a hundred years later, stating: "He tenaciously and patiently and lucidly made his way through the whole South, undiscouraged by churlish natives, almost impassable roads or the cold inns and uncomfortable cabins in which he spent most of his nights. He talked to everybody and he sized up everything, and he wrote it all down."[30]

WRITING THE SOUTH

Olmsted's columns on his second trip, this time called "A Tour in the Southwest," numbered only fifteen and ran in the *Daily News* from March to June 1854. Though that trip was twice as long and his notes nearly as voluminous, what appeared in print amounted to less than a third of the newspaper's coverage of his first trip. One reason seems to be that interest in Texas was waning as Kansas and Nebraska took center stage in the national consciousness. Illinois senator Stephen Douglas's proposal to organize both as territories triggered new debate, particularly over the issue of shifting the decision as to their status as slave or free away from Congress to the people settling those territories, under the principle of "popular sovereignty." The violence that erupted as a result of the Kansas-Nebraska Act of 1854, especially in the ruthless vendettas that bred the term "Bleeding Kansas," along with other political developments, led to the emergence later that year of a new party, the Republicans, committed to a "free-soil" agenda. As a result, the space that Raymond might otherwise have devoted to his southern correspondent's Texas and "back country" reports gave way to coverage of more immediate concerns. Eventually, Olmsted would publish a series of ten articles on the final leg of his 1854 journey in a rival paper, the *New York Tribune*, in the summer of 1857, but it was the transposition of those writings to book form that by then claimed most of Olmsted's energy and effort.[31]

Olmsted had in mind the idea of book-length narratives of his southern travels even before he solidified his agreement to serve as a correspondent for the *Daily News*. He confided to a friend in October 1852: "I have thoughts of going South this winter . . . mainly with the idea that

I could make a valuable book of observations on Southern Agriculture & general economy as affected by slavery."[32] As early as January 1853, he asked his father to edit his newspaper columns both for style and factual accuracy, thinking they would need considerable revision before appearing in book form.[33] Soon after his final return from the South, he began to revise his work himself, adding statistical and historical data to substantiate the dispatches he had somewhat hastily compiled from his notes while on the move.

With his father's financial backing, he published his first volume in January 1856 under the title *A Journey in the Seaboard Slave States*, and with his own name as author, rather than the anonymous "Yeoman" used for his newspaper columns. At more than seven hundred pages (in two volumes), it was the first book-length work produced by the fledgling firm Dix & Edwards, named for two young men who up to that point had published only magazines and journals. They invited Olmsted not only to publish with them but also to become a partner in the firm, and he was immediately drawn to the venture and to the literary world into which it gave him entrée. The book was well received by critics, although both its size and its cost (at $1.25, the price was five times as high as that for *Walks and Talks*) made for slow sales at first. Sales were soon boosted by its reception abroad, however, where it was published in London by Sampson Low, Son & Company, which would go on to publish all of Olmsted's volumes and, ultimately, their condensation as *The Cotton Kingdom*.

A year later, Dix & Edwards published Olmsted's much-expanded account of his second journey, titled *A Journey through Texas; or, a Saddle-Trip on the Southwestern Frontier*. Much of the work in pulling it together had fallen to John Hull, given that Olmsted's energies were directed at expanding Dix & Edwards's markets in Europe. Also highly praised but with only modest sales, it was, according to Olmsted, "my best book . . . because edited by my brother."[34] John succumbed to his tuberculosis just before it appeared early in 1857; two years later, Fred married his widow, Mary.

The final volume of Olmsted's southern trilogy, titled *A Journey in the Back Country*, was slower in coming, due in part to the fact that he did not have completed dispatches to work from, only notes he had made during the trip. Other responsibilities also slowed Olmsted down. He spent much of 1856 in Europe, traveling for Dix & Edwards, but the publishing house met its demise during the Panic of 1857, for which Olmsted, as a partner, took a financial hit as well. Later that year, he accepted the position of superintendent of New York City's newly established Central Park. Thus it was only in the summer of 1860 that the third volume of his southern chronicles finally appeared, produced by a new publisher, Mason Brothers.

By the time *A Journey in the Back Country* was published, the presidential election was well under way, and there were ominous signs that the sectional crisis might reach a breaking point depending on the election's outcome. Olmsted had become increasingly engaged in sectional politics since his ventures south and had taken a particularly active role in encouraging and financially supporting the movement of free-soil settlers in the embroiled Kansas Territory. Once Lincoln's election in November triggered southern threats of secession, Olmsted became alarmed about the breakdown of the Union and embraced military force to prevent it. "My mind is made up for a fight," he confided to Charles Brace early in December. "The sooner we get used to the idea the better, I think."[35] With that comment, Olmsted all but acknowledged that his writings and other efforts exerting moderating influences in the clash between North and South had proved futile. Subsequently, he worked to rally support for the Union and to stem the tide of secession that swept the South, beginning with South Carolina's withdrawal from the United States in December 1860 (followed by six other Deep South states in January 1861) and culminating in the formation of a Confederate government in early February.

As the crisis intensified, the role of Great Britain became a source of speculation and concern. From his own visits there, Olmsted was fully aware of Britain's aversion to American slavery. Yet he also realized, as did many southerners, that many industrialists and other powerful voices in the British government backed the new southern nation, and he recognized the diplomatic and economic opportunities afforded by a divided America. The demand for southern cotton to fuel the British textile industry proved especially encouraging to Confederate leaders who had high hopes for a formal alliance with and wartime support from their premier trading partner abroad.

Early in 1861, Olmsted's British publisher, Sampson Low, offered him a chance to counter those efforts through his writings. His editors there proposed a much-abridged single-volume edition of his southern trilogy that would be published primarily for a British market. They sensed correctly that interest in the South and slavery was at its height and that it would be a good time to expose to a wider readership, and in more accessible form, the work of the man many in Britain viewed as the leading authority on both. Sampson Low agreed to allow Olmsted's New York publisher, Mason Brothers, to release an American edition of the book soon after their own volume appeared.

Because Olmsted was fully engaged in his work at Central Park and time was of the essence, he hired a North Carolina native and anti-slavery advocate named Daniel Goodloe, then editor of a Washington, D.C., newspaper, to help him produce this new iteration of his slavery chronicles. Olmsted and Goodloe agreed that the easiest way to perform such radical surgery on the trilogy was to eliminate most of the material on Texas (only about an eighth of it, mostly focusing on east Texas, was retained) and about half of the recently published *A Journey in the Back Country*. Olmsted insisted on adding material—often updated statistical and other economic data—along with further commentary on a number of themes and issues touched on in the original books.

He chose the title *The Cotton Kingdom*, playing off a much-quoted speech made before Congress in 1858 by South Carolina senator James Henry Hammond, in which Hammond announced that in world, as in national, affairs, "cotton is king." Hammond claimed that if cotton imports ended, "England would topple headlong and carry the whole civilized world with her save the South. No! You dare not make war upon cotton."[36] Olmsted's title is purposefully ironic in that the thrust of the volume, and a theme pointedly laid out in a new introduction, was that cotton was not nearly so powerful a force as Hammond's arrogance suggested and certainly not a reason for Britain to back the new Confederacy.

With Goodloe's help, Olmsted shipped the manuscript overseas in June. Sampson Low began typesetting it almost immediately and had bound copies of the book ready for sale by October. The final product came in at 768 pages, divided into two volumes. A month later, the Masons had their edition available for American readers. If *The Cotton Kingdom*'s impact was somewhat blunted because it appeared in the fall of 1861, well after the outbreak of the Civil War in April, it sold reasonably well in the United States and Britain (outselling all three of the volumes from which it was derived) and was critically acclaimed in both countries. The New England poet and critic James Russell Lowell told Olmsted, "I have learned more about the South from your books than from all others put together, and I value them the more that an American who can be patient and accurate is so rare a phenomenon."[37] Even as staunch an antislavery advocate as Harriet Beecher Stowe, an acquaintance of Olmsted's, conceded that it was "the most thorough exposé of the economical view of this subject [slavery] which has ever appeared."[38] The Boston academic Charles Eliot Norton provided perhaps the most profuse recommendation of Olmsted's work, calling his collective output "the most important contributions to an exact acquaintance with the conditions and results of slavery in this country that have ever been published. They have permanent value, and will be chief material for our social history whenever it is written."[39]

On the other side of the Atlantic, *The Cotton Kingdom* made a significant impression on prominent British opinion makers. Intellectuals such as Charles Dickens, John Stuart Mill, and Charles Darwin endorsed it as the most reliable and useful account of southern slavery and society in print. Darwin's wife, Emma, saw its potential in mobilizing her countrymen's opposition to slavery and the Confederacy. She confided to a friend, "About America I think the slaves are gradually getting freed & that is what I chiefly care for. . . . I think all England has to read up Olmsted's works & get up its Uncle Tom again."[40]

ASSESSING THE SOUTH

When Charles Brace moved on to Germany after parting ways with the Olmsted brothers in England back in 1851, and subsequently decided to write an account of his travels there, Olmsted offered his friend some advice that reveals much about his own approach to depicting the South for the reading public. "Why not tell us about what you *did, saw*, and *said*, and what was said by others?" Olmsted suggested. "You should be able to state personal interviews, conversations, observations of particular persons and things; personal adventures, usages, superstitions, &c., &c. that would be valuable to [political journalist Horace] Greeley as well as interesting to Aunt Maria."[41] In essence, this is how Olmsted documented the South. As one scholar phrased it, "His study of conditions was practical rather than theoretical, realistic rather than emotional."[42] It was that approach that accounts for much of the success of his writings in terms of readers' response at the time, as well as its enduring value for readers today. At the same time, his lack of emotional engagement, intentional as it was, fails to convey the far more impassioned rhetoric that typified most such contemporary commentary in both the North and the South.

What distinguished Olmsted's writings from most travelers' accounts of the South is that he was among the few charged specifically with examining slavery and its relationship to the southern economy and society and with conveying those realities to a broad northern readership.

From the outset, his determination to take in all facets of southern life and labor was apparent, as his first dispatches from Virginia demonstrate. He interspersed throughout his more general assessments considerable anecdotal data—stories, character sketches, and other vivid accounts of particular incidents and people. He deemed no encounter, interview, or observation unworthy of his attention or of several pages of commentary.

He also took advantage of his various modes of travel and the range of hosts and fellow guests whom he met on his journeys, incorporating into his narrative conversations with slave traders, merchants, emigrants, overseers, and foremen, as well as slaves, free blacks, and a host of poor whites, who ranged from settlers on the Texas frontier to southern highlanders in Appalachia. His contacts, as Edmund Wilson later described them, included "people who are courteous and people who are oafish, men who think slavery a curse and men who think it ordained by Heaven, masters who mistreat their slaves and masters who take excellent care of them; many gradations of misery and squalor, and a few of relative comfort."[43] Rare was the chronicler so willing to give "equal time" to such a vast a range of viewpoints on what had become by then so polarizing an issue.

Although the original intent of his mission was to focus on agriculture, Olmsted spent relatively little time on plantations. He carried with him only a handful of letters of introduction to planters and failed to make contact with several of them. While he made the most of his visits to the few plantations—tobacco, rice, sugar, and cotton—where planters received him and allowed him full access and explanation of their operations, perhaps it was the many missed opportunities for such onsite inspections that made him focus as much attention on cities, towns, small farms, and even remote sparsely settled areas as he did on the vast cash crop enterprises that most nonsoutherners saw as the region's essence.

Despite the seeming randomness—or indiscriminate inclusiveness—of this Connecticut Yankee's coverage of what he saw and heard, observations regarding slavery dominated his reports, and certain themes emerged early and were sustained throughout. Even as Olmsted sought to maintain the objectivity that he and his employer Henry Raymond touted in introducing his series, his own racial and class prejudices are evident throughout his commentary and readily apparent to readers today.

For example, Olmsted was careful to avoid harsh criticism of slaveholders' treatment of their African American property. He was often susceptible to the sanitized versions of plantation life that his hosts chose to present to him. This seems to have been especially true during his first trip, that along the eastern seaboard. Though he later developed a more skeptical approach to what he saw and heard from his planter hosts, he admitted at one point that their hospitality toward this northern observer was in hindsight a deliberate attempt to show off their plantation operations to best advantage, while shielding him from their worst abuses (not that he ever seemed to have made much of an effort to seek out such abuses).[44] As one biographer stated, "He considered the South not wicked, slaveholders not necessarily bad; slavery was the entailed misfortune of the section, and a slave's master could be as good a Christian as a Yankee."[45]

Olmsted expressed only slight sympathy for the slaves he encountered, and he gave only occasional lip service to the inhumanity and exploitation inherent in the system. It is significant that he never visited a slave market or attended a slave auction—or at least never wrote of these experiences—despite having spent several days in New Orleans, Mobile, and other Deep South cities in which such activities were prevalent.[46] By avoiding such sites and the topic in general, Olmsted also managed to avoid acknowledging one of the system's cruelest and most emotionally wrenching realities, and the one most frequently emphasized by abolitionists: the splitting of families—husbands from wives, and parents, especially mothers, from children. Even in what are often quite revealing discussions with individual African Americans, Olmsted chose to engage only with free blacks or slaves in somewhat privileged positions and portrayed them less as victims than as resourceful individuals who made the most of their circumstances.[47] Perhaps his emphasis on slaves' religious activity also served to deflect attention away from their plight by touting—as their owners themselves often did—what was arguably one of the more tangible benefits of slavery as an institution.

If Olmsted eschewed the moral high ground that he so abhorred in abolitionist rhetoric, he readily found much to fault in terms of the practicality and profitability of slave labor. Most notably, he stressed the economic inefficiency of black bondage and its stifling of both agricultural diversity and industrial development throughout the region. "The negroes are a degraded people," he wrote, "degraded not merely by position, but actually immoral and low-lived; without healthy ambition; but little influenced by high moral considerations, and in regard to labor, not at all affected by regard to duty."[48] In effect, he seemed to find slaves themselves culpable for their low moral standards and lack of a work ethic, the latter one of the major factors contributing to the economic inefficiency of the system.

Far more than his fellow commentators on the antebellum South, Olmsted was exposed to the considerable range of nonplantation enterprises that utilized slave labor. In describing them as well as the more familiar agricultural venues in which slaves worked, he stressed not only the inefficiency of their efforts but also the fact that slave labor shut out opportunities for gainful employment among white laborers. Some of this was by choice: "No white man," he observed, "would ever do certain kinds of work (such as taking care of cattle, or getting water or wood to be used in the house), and if you should ask a white man you had hired to do such things, he would get mad and tell you he wasn't a nigger."[49]

Olmsted also stressed the fact that slavery discouraged any efforts to generate a more diversified agricultural output, which would have freed planters of their dependency on, and exploitation by, the northern middlemen who controlled the cotton and tobacco markets within which they had to sell their crops. He challenged a Carolina planter on this point, telling him, "I have raised hay, potatoes, and cabbages on my farm in New York, that found a market in Richmond, but you have capital soil for such crops; how is it you don't supply your own markets?" To which the planter replied: "I should be laughed at if I bothered with such small crops." Olmsted scoffed at such shortsightedness, noting that southern farmers "leave such little crops for the niggers and Yankees, and then grumble because all the profits of their business go to build 'Fifth-avenue palaces' and 'down-east school houses.'"[50]

If detachment and relative objectivity were both goals and trademarks of the original volumes, Olmsted had a more specific agenda when he abridged those three books to create *The Cotton Kingdom*. While the tone of his coverage remained largely the same as in those volumes—or, indeed, as in his newspaper columns of nearly a decade earlier—his newly composed introduction, "The Present Crisis," made clear that he intended his testimonials as a means to sway the British people to avoid any investment in or commitment to the Confederate cause. There was nothing conciliatory or ambivalent about his message this time. Now that the North and South were at war, a war that would ultimately determine the fate of slavery and the economy it upheld, it was imperative that the South must be subjugated. He argued that the South's prospects for winning this war were much weakened by their dependence on cotton and on slavery. Not only was the southern cause weak, even doomed, Olmsted insisted, it was also misguided. Only by slavery's destruction would that society itself ever break free of the shackles that so limited its prospects in an ever-modernizing world. He saw his own observations and experiences as laid out in *The Cotton Kingdom* as vivid testimony as to why this was the case, and yet here again, as in the original volumes, the abuses the system inflicted on its true victims received only fleeting acknowledgment in his assessment of why slavery needed to be eradicated.

OLMSTED'S LATER LIFE AND CAREER

Even as his books on the South were making their way into print, Olmsted's career as a writer had given way to another enterprise for which he is most widely remembered today—that of America's preeminent landscape architect. From mid-1857 until the war broke out, he served as superintendent of New York City's Central Park, overseeing with his partner in the project, architect Calvert Vaux, its design and construction. In so doing, one critic claimed, Olmsted "invented the American park at a time when large public gardens had been thought to be too aristocratic to be sanctioned in America, too artistic to be respected by the American populace."[51]

During the war, Olmsted moved to Washington to serve as the general secretary of the U.S. Sanitary Commission, a private agency that recruited thousands of volunteers to work in hospitals established throughout the North and in war zones throughout the South to treat sick and wounded Union soldiers. In 1863, he made yet another seemingly radical career decision when he accepted an invitation to move to California to manage the Mariposa Company, a financially troubled gold-mining enterprise established in the late 1840s by John C. Frémont. Olmsted spent the last year and a half of the war there, but he was unable to overcome the problems that kept the operation from being profitable and thus was more than ready to return east at war's end. Perhaps the biggest impact on Olmsted's future ventures was the time he spent in the Sierra Nevada and Yosemite Valley, both located near the Mariposa mining operations, which gave him an even greater appreciation for nature's scenic beauty and the need to preserve it.

Olmsted returned to his work with Vaux on Central Park. Both also took on a similar project for nearby Brooklyn, which resulted in its equally impressive Prospect Park. Over the next two decades, the scope and range of Olmsted's output was extraordinary. He designed dozens of public parks, residential neighborhoods, and cemeteries in cities and towns across America, as well as numerous college campuses, including the University of Chicago; the University of California, Berkeley; and Stanford University. Olmsted created Boston's Back Bay by draining sewage-infested marshland and adding landfill that supported both public parks and eventually an extensive residential area. He designed the grounds of the U.S. Capitol in Washington, including the grand marble staircases and terraces that define the approach to the hilltop edifice. He became a strong advocate for conservation and proved an influential advocate for establishing America's first state park, Niagara Falls (1885), and its second national park, Yosemite (1890).

Only occasionally did Olmsted's work take him back to the South. In 1888, George Washington Vanderbilt, the twenty-six-year-old heir to one of the nation's largest family fortunes, hired Olmsted to design a vast private park that would encompass the more than two thousand acres he had purchased in the Blue Ridge Mountains just outside Asheville, North Carolina, and on which he built the largest private residence in America—the famed Biltmore House. This was an area Olmsted remembered from 1854, when he had traveled through North Carolina and stayed in Asheville. "There is no experience of my life to which I could return with more satisfaction," he told Vanderbilt. Because he recalled specifically the beautiful woodlands that made up so much of the antebellum Appalachian landscape, and because of the strong environmentalist sensibility he had developed in the years since, Olmsted convinced Vanderbilt to leave much of the estate forested, rather than turn it all into formal gardens and parks resembling those at Versailles and other European palaces, as his young employer had originally envisioned.[52] The model forest he planned and implemented there—which ultimately spread over more than 100,000 acres—set a precedent for modern forest management and led to the creation of the nation's first school of forestry, founded on Vanderbilt land only a few miles from the family's magnificent home.

Olmsted spent much of the early 1890s working on the Biltmore Estate, while taking on other southern projects as well, including designing the campus of Auburn University in Alabama and developing an early suburb of Atlanta called Druid Hills. One of his final projects was his design of the grounds of the Chicago World's Fair in 1893. Two years later, in 1895, he began to suffer from senility, and by 1898 he was institutionalized in a Massachusetts hospital, the grounds of which he had designed years earlier. He remained there until his death in 1903.

Olmsted's biographer Justin Martin suggests that "his life and career were just too sprawling and spectacular" for a focus on any one aspect of them to do him justice. "Ask people today about Olmsted," he writes, "and they're likely to come back with a few details—best case. Olmsted may well be the most important American historical figure that the average person knows least about."[53] That may well be true, but for scholars of southern history and of slavery, his name and his journalistic output will always loom large.

NOTES

[1] The first volume, *A Journey in the Seaboard Slave States* (New York, 1856), chronicles the entirety of Olmsted's first trip, while the latter two volumes describe different legs of his second trip, as indicated by their respective titles, *A Journey through Texas; or, A Saddle Trip on the Southwestern Frontier* (New York, 1857) and *A Journey in the Back Country in the Winter of 1853–54*, 2 vols.(New York, 1860), which is why references here and elsewhere are to his *three* southern trips, rather than just two.

[2] Two recent studies of such accounts are John D. Cox, *Traveling South: Travel Narratives and the Construction of American Identity* (Athens, Ga., 2005), and Joe Lockard, *Watching Slavery: Witness Texts and Travel Reports* (New York, 2008).

[3] The best overview of fugitive slave narratives remains William L. Andrews, *To Tell a Free Story: The First Century of Afro-American Autobiography, 1760–1865* (Urbana, Ill., 1986). The best collection of such works is William L. Andrews and Henry Louis Gates Jr., eds., *The Civitas Anthology of African American Slave Narratives* (Washington, D.C., 1999).

[4] On the Grimké sisters, see Gerda Lerner, *The Sarah and Angelina Grimké Sisters from South Carolina: Pioneers for Women's Rights and Abolition* (1971; repr., Chapel Hill, N.C., 1998), and Mark E. Perry, *Lift Up Thy Voice: The Grimké Family's Journey from Slaveholders to Civil Rights Leaders* (New York, 2002). On Fanny Kemble, see her *Journal of a Residence on a Georgian Plantation, 1838–1839* (New York, 1863), and Catherine Clinton, *Fanny Kemble's Civil Wars* (New York, 2000). On Levi Coffin, see his *Reminiscences* (Cincinnati, 1876); George and Willene Hendrick, eds., *Fleeing for Freedom; Stories of the Underground Railroad, as Told by Levi Coffin and William Still* (Chicago, 2004); and Mary Ann Yannessa, *Levi Coffin, Quaker: Breaking the Bonds of Slavery in Ohio and Indiana* (Richmond, Ind., 2001).

[5] James L. Huston, "The Experiential Basis of the Northern Antislavery Impulse," *Journal of Southern History* 50 (1990): 609–40.

[6] See James Redpath, *The Roving Editor; or, Talks with Slaves in the Southern States*, ed. John R. McKivigan (1859; repr., University Park, Pa., 1996), and John R. McKivigan, *Forgotten Firebrand: James Redpath and the Making of Nineteenth-Century America* (Ithaca, N.Y., 2008).

[7] Theodore Dwight Weld, *American Slavery as It Is: Testimony of a Thousand Witnesses* (1839; repr., Chapel Hill, N.C., 2011).

[8] C. G. Parsons, *Inside View of Slavery: or, A Tour among the Planters* (1855; repr., Savannah, Ga., 1974), 53.

[9] Karl Bernhard, Duke of Saxe-Weimar-Eisenach, *Travels through North America, during the Years 1825 and 1826*, 2 vols. (Philadelphia, 1828); Frederika Bremer, *The Homes of the New World: Impressions of America* (New York, 1853); Sir Charles Lyell, *A Second Visit to the United States of North America*, 2 vols. (New York, 1849); George W. Featherstonhaugh, *Excursion through the Slave States, from Washington on the Potomac to the Frontier of Mexico* (New York, 1844); Harriet Martineau, *Society in America* (London, 1837); James Silk Buckingham, *The Slave States of America*, 2 vols. (London, 1842). For overviews of these works and others, see Max Berger, "American Slavery as Seen by British Visitors, 1836–1860," *Journal of Negro History* 30 (April 1945): 181–202, and Eugene H. Berwanger, *As They Saw Slavery* (Minneapolis, 1973).

[10] Frederick Law Olmsted, "Autobiographical Fragment B," ca. mid-1870s, in *The Papers of Frederick Law Olmsted*, vol. 1, *The Formative Years, 1822–1852*, ed. Charles

Capen McLaughlin and Charles E. Beveridge (Baltimore, 1977), 115 (hereafter cited as *Papers of Olmsted*).
[11] Olmsted, "Autobiographical Fragment: Passages in the Life of an Unpractical Man," in *Papers of Olmsted*, 1:100. Olmsted has been the subject of several biographies, including Broadus Mitchell, *Frederick Law Olmsted: A Critic of the Old South* (Baltimore, 1924); Laura Wood Roper, *FLO: A Biography of Frederick Law Olmsted* (Baltimore, 1973); John Emerson Todd, *Frederick Law Olmsted* (Boston, 1982); Lee Hall, *Olmsted's America: An "Unpractical" Man and His Vision of Civilization* (Boston, 1995); Witold Rybczynski, *A Clearing in the Distance: Frederick Law Olmsted and America in the Nineteenth Century* (New York, 1999); and Justin Martin, *Genius of Place: The Life of Frederick Law Olmsted* (Cambridge, Mass., 2011).
[12] Introduction to *Papers of Olmsted*, 1:4–5; Roper, *FLO*, chap. 1.
[13] Hall, *Olmsted's America*, 17.
[14] Olmsted, "A Voice from the Sea," *American Whig Review* 14 (December 1851). Olmsted began writing this essay six years after the events he recounted while on his next voyage, in 1850, en route to Liverpool, where he began his walking tour of England.
[15] Harvey Wish, ed., introduction to *The Slave States*, by Frederick Law Olmsted (New York, 1959), 9.
[16] Hall, *Olmsted's America*, 40.
[17] Roper, *FLO*, 83–84.
[18] Quoted in ibid., 84.
[19] Olmsted to Frederick Kingsbury, October 17, 1852, in *Papers of Olmsted*, vol. 2., *Slavery and the South, 1852–1857*, ed. McLaughlin and Beveridge (Baltimore, 1981), 83.
[20] Olmsted, *A Journey in the Back Country*, 1: vi.
[21] Ibid., 1: vi–vii.
[22] Ibid., 1: ix–x. See also Mitchell, *Frederick Law Olmsted*, 69–70.
[23] Martin, *Genius of Place*, 77.
[24] Olmsted to Kingsbury, October 17, 1852, in *Papers of Olmsted*, 2: 83.
[25] Appendix 2 in *Papers of Olmsted*, 2: 467–71, consists of a day-by-day itinerary of Olmsted's first trip through the South.
[26] Quoted in Arthur M. Schlesinger, ed., introduction to *The Cotton Kingdom: A Traveller's Observations on Cotton & Slavery in the American Slave States*, by Frederick Law Olmsted (New York, 1953), xvii–xviii.
[27] Ibid., xix.
[28] Appendix 2 in *Papers of Olmsted*, 2: 471–70, consists of a day-by-day itinerary of Olmsted's trip through Texas.
[29] Ibid., 480–82. While that itinerary treats Olmsted's journeys through Texas and then through the "back country" as a single journey, labeling it simply the "Second Southern Journey," Olmsted himself and most scholars since have viewed these as two distinct trips, perhaps because they were covered in separate volumes, published three years apart.
[30] Edmund Wilson, *Patriotic Gore: Studies in the Literature of the American Civil War* (New York, 1962), 221.
[31] Schlesinger, introduction, xix–xx.
[32] Olmsted to Kingsbury, October 17, 1852, in *Papers of Olmsted*, 2: 82.
[33] Mitchell, *Frederick Law Olmsted*, 47.
[34] Martin, *Genius of Place*, 120.
[35] Olmsted to Brace, December 8, 1860, quoted in Mitchell, *Frederick Law Olmsted*, 54.
[36] Quoted in Martin, *Genius of Place*, 208.
[37] James Russell Lowell to Frederick Law Olmsted, January 25, 1862, quoted in Todd, *Frederick Law Olmsted*, 66.
[38] Quoted in Schlesinger, introduction, xxvi.
[39] Quoted in Roper, *FLO*, 152.
[40] Quoted in Martin, *Genius of Place*, 208.

[41] Quoted in Mitchell, *Frederick Law Olmsted*, 46.

[42] Schlesinger, introduction, xxi.

[43] Wilson, *Patriotic Gore*, 224.

[44] See, for example, his reference to a Georgia rice plantation he visited as a "show plantation" in Selection 15.

[45] Roper, *FLO*, 85.

[46] The one exception is a description of an auction in Richmond, which Olmsted published as "The Slave Trade in Virginia" in *Chambers' Journal* (October 1853) and Schlesinger included as appendix B in his edition of *The Cotton Kingdom*.

[47] See, for example, Selections 14, 17, and 37.

[48] Olmsted, *A Journey in the Seaboard Slave States*, 209.

[49] Ibid., 82–83.

[50] Quoted in Rybczynski, *A Clearing in the Wilderness*, 114.

[51] Wilson, *Patriotic Gore*, 219.

[52] Martin, *Genius of Place*, 362–64.

[53] Ibid., 1.

PART TWO

Selections from
The Cotton Kingdom

Introduction

"The Present Crisis"

This introduction to The Cotton Kingdom *is the only part of the book that was originally written in 1861. Though Olmsted never explicitly explained his purpose or his methods in putting together this condensation of his earlier writings, it is clear from these introductory remarks what his agenda was: an appeal specifically to British readers in which he refuted the southern claim that "cotton is king" and offered instead a more factually based assessment of the vulnerability of the South's cotton economy and of the labor force on which it depended. The Civil War had begun by the time Olmsted wrote this introduction, and he wanted the British to know that this was to be a war of "subjugation"—a term he used repeatedly to convey the determination with which the North must pursue the conflict in order to destroy slavery. If it failed, the South would prevail and, in so doing, subjugate the values on which the American nation was built—values inherited from its mother country.*

Only the beginning and closing sections of the introduction are included here. This is about a third of the whole, which ran for twenty-seven pages in the original edition.

The mountain ranges, the valleys, and the great waters of America, all trend north and south, not east and west. An arbitrary political line may divide the north part from the south part, but there is no such line in nature: there can be none, socially. While water runs downhill, the currents and counter currents of trade, of love, of consanguinity, and fellowship, will flow north and south. The unavoidable comminglings of the people in a land like this, upon the conditions which the slavery of a portion of the population impose, make it necessary to peace that we should all live under the same laws and respect the same flag.

No government could long control its own people, no government could long exist, that would allow its citizens to be subject to such indignities under a foreign government as those to which the citizens of the United States heretofore have been required to submit under their own, for the sake of the tranquility of the South. Nor could the South, with its present purposes, live on terms of peace with any foreign nation, between whose people and its own there was no division, except such an one as might be maintained by means of forts, frontier-guards and custom-houses, edicts, passports and spies. Scotland, Wales, and Ireland are each much better adapted for an independent government, and under an independent government would be far more likely to live at peace with England, than the South to remain peaceably separated from the North of this country.

It is said that the South can never be subjugated. It must be, or we must. It must be, or not only our American republic is a failure, but our English justice and our English law and our English freedom are failures. This Southern repudiation of obligations upon the result of an election [the presidential election of 1860] is but a clearer warning than we have had before, that these cannot be maintained in this land any longer in such intimate association with slavery as we have hitherto tried to hope that they might. We now know that we must give them up, or give up trying to accommodate ourselves to what the South has declared, and demonstrated, to be the necessities of its state of society. Those necessities would not be less, but, on the contrary, far more imperative were the South an independent people. If the South has reason to declare itself independent of our long-honoured constitution, and of our common court or our common laws, on account of a past want of invariable tenderness on the part of each one of our people towards its necessities, how long could we calculate to be able to preserve ourselves from occurrences which would be deemed to abrogate the obligations of a mere treaty of peace? A treaty of peace with the South as a foreign power, would be a cowardly armistice, a cruel aggravation and prolongation of war.

Subjugation! I do not choose the word, but take it, and use it in the only sense in which it can be applicable. This is a Republic, and the South must come under the yoke of freedom, not to work for us, but to work with us, on equal terms, as a free people. To work with us, for the security of a state of society, the ruling purpose and tendency of which, [in] spite of all its bendings heretofore, to the necessities of slavery; spite of the incongruous foreign elements which it has had constantly to absorb and incorporate; spite of a strong element of excessive backwoods individualism, has, beyond all question, been favourable to sound and safe progress in knowledge, civilization, and Christianity.

To this yoke the head of the South must now be lifted, or we must bend our necks to that of slavery. . . . One system or the other is to thrive and extend, and eventually possess and govern this whole land.

This has been long felt and acted upon at the South; and the purpose of the more prudent and conservative men, now engaged in the attempt to establish a new government in the South, was for a long time simply to obtain an advantage for what was talked of as "reconstruction"; namely, a process of change in the form and rules of our government that would disqualify us of the Free States from offering any resistance to whatever was demanded of our government, for the end in view of the extension and eternal maintenance of slavery. . . . That the true people of the United States could have allowed the mutiny to proceed so far, before rising in their strength to resist it, is due chiefly to the instinctive reliance which every grumbler really gets to have under our forms of society, in the ultimate common-sense of the great body of the people, and to the incredulity with which the report has been regarded, that slavery had made such a vast difference between the character of the South and that of the country at large. Few were fully convinced that the whole proceedings of the insurgents meant anything else than a more than usually bold and scandalous way of playing the game of brag, to which we had been so long used in our politics, and of which the people of England had a little experience shortly before the passage of a certain Reform Bill. The instant effect of the first *shotted*-gun that was fired [at Fort Sumter] proves this. We knew then that we had to subjugate slavery, or be subjugated by it.

Peace is now not possible until the people of the South are well convinced that the form of society, to fortify which is the ostensible purpose of the war into which they have been plunged, is not worth fighting for, or until we think the sovereignty of our convictions of Justice, Freedom, Law and the conditions of Civilization in this land to be of less worth than the lives and property of our generation.

From the St. Lawrence to the Mexican Gulf, freedom must everywhere give way to the necessities of slavery, or slavery must be accommodated to the necessary incidents of freedom.

Where the hopes and sympathies of Englishmen will be, we well know.

"The necessity to labour is incompatible with a high civilization, with heroic spirit in those subject to it."

"The institution of African slavery is a means more effective than any other yet devised, for relieving a large body of men from the necessity of labour; consequently, states which possess it must be stronger in statesmanship and in war, than those which do not; especially must they be stronger than states in which there is absolutely no privileged class, but all men are held to be equal before the law."

"The civilized world is dependent upon the Slave States of America for a supply of cotton. The demand for this commodity has, during many years, increased faster than the supply. Sales are made of it, now, to the amount of two hundred millions of dollars in a year, yet they have a vast area of soil suitable for its production which has never been broken. . . . The world must have cotton, and the world depends on them for it. Whatever they demand, that must be conceded them; whatever they want, they have but to stretch forth their hands and take it."

These fallacies, lodged in certain minds, generated, long ago, grand ambitions, and bold schemes of conquest and wealth. The people of the North stood in the way of these schemes. In the minds of the schemers, labour had been associated with servility, meekness, cowardice; and they were persuaded that all men not degraded by labour at the North "kept aloof from politics," or held their judgment in entire subjection to the daily wants of a working population, of no more spirit and no more patriotism than their own working men — slaves. They believed this whole people to be really in a state of dependence, and that they controlled that upon which they depended.

So, to a hitherto vague and inert local partisanship, they brought a purpose of determination to overcome the North, and, as this could not be safely avowed, there was the necessity for a conspiracy, and for the cloak of a conspiracy. By means the most mendacious, the ignorant, proud, jealous, and violent free population of the cotton States and their dependencies, were persuaded that less consideration was paid to their political demands than the importance of their contentment entitled them to expect from their government, and were at length decoyed into a state of angry passion, in which they only needed leaders of sufficient audacity to bring them into open rebellion. Assured that their own power if used would be supreme, and that they had but to offer sufficient evidence of a violent and dangerous determination to overawe the sordid North, and make it submit to a "reconstruction" of the nation in a form more advantageous to themselves, they were artfully led along in a constant advance, and constant failure of attempts at intimidation, until at length they must needs take part in a desperate rebellion, or accept a position which, after the declarations they had made for the purpose of intimidation, they could not do without humiliation. . . .

"No! you dare not make war upon cotton; no power on earth dares to make war upon it. Cotton is king; until lately the Bank of England was king; but she tried to put her screws, as usual, the fall before the last, on the cotton crop, and was utterly vanquished. The last power has been conquered: who can doubt, that has looked at recent events, that cotton is supreme?"

These are the defiant and triumphant words of Governor [James Henry] Hammond, of South Carolina, addressed to the Senate of the

United States, March 4th, 1858. Almost every important man of the South, has at one time or other, within a few years, been betrayed into the utterance of similar exultant anticipations; and the South would never have been led into the great and terrible mistake it has made, had it not been for this confident conviction in the minds of the men who have been passing for its statesmen. Whatever moral strength the rebellion has, abroad or at home, lies chiefly in the fact that this conviction is also held, more or less distinctly, by multitudes who know perfectly well that the commonly assigned reasons for it are based on falsehoods.

Recently, a banker, who is and always has been a loyal union man, said, commenting upon certain experiences of mine narrated in this book: "The South cannot be poor. Why, their last crop alone was worth two hundred million. They must be rich": ergo, say the conspirators, adopting the same careless conclusion, they must be powerful, and the world must feel their power, and respect them and their institutions.

My own observation of the real condition of the people of our Slave States, gave me, on the contrary, an impression that the cotton monopoly in some way did them more harm than good; and, although the written narration of what I saw was not intended to set this forth, upon reviewing it for the present publication, I find the impression has become a conviction. I propose here, therefore, to show how the main body of the observations of the book arrange themselves in my mind with reference to this question. . . .

Coming directly from my farm in New York to Eastern Virginia, I was satisfied, after a few weeks' observation, that the most of the people lived very poorly; that the proportion of men improving their condition was much less than in any Northern community; and that the natural resources of the land were strangely unused, or were used with poor economy. . . .

. . .

One of the grand errors, out of which this rebellion has grown, came from supposing that whatever nourishes wealth and gives power to an ordinary civilized community must command as much for a slave-holding community. The truth has been overlooked that the accumulation of wealth and the power of a nation are contingent not merely upon the primary value of the surplus of productions of which it has to dispose, but very largely also upon the way in which the income from its surplus is distributed and reinvested. Let a man be absent from almost any part of the North twenty years, and he is struck, on his return, by what we call the "improvements" which have been made. Better buildings, churches, school-houses, mills, railroads, etc. In New York city alone, for instance, at least two hundred millions of dollars have been reinvested merely in an improved housing of the people; in labour-saving machinery, waterworks, gasworks, etc., as much more. It is not difficult to see where the profits of our manufacturers and merchants are. Again, go into the country, and there is no end of substantial proof of twenty years of agricultural prosperity, not alone in roads, canals, bridges, dwellings, barns and fences, but in books and furniture, and gardens, and pictures, and in the better dress and evidently higher education of the people.

But where will the returning traveller see the accumulated cotton profits of twenty years in Mississippi? Ask the cotton-planter for them, and he will point in reply, not to dwellings, libraries, churches, school-houses, mills, railroads, or anything of the kind; he will point to his negroes—to almost nothing else. Negroes such as stood for five hundred dollars once, now represent a thousand dollars. We must look then in Virginia and those Northern Slave States which have the monopoly of supplying negroes, for the real wealth which the sale of cotton has brought to the South. But where is the evidence of it? where anything to compare with the evidence of accumulated profits to be seen in any Free State? If certain portions of Virginia have been a little improving, others unquestionably have been deteriorating, growing shabbier, more comfortless, less convenient. The total increase in wealth of the population during the last twenty years shows for almost nothing. One year's improvements of a Free State exceed it all.

Chapter 1

Virginia and the Carolinas

On December 10, 1852, after a twelve-hour train ride from New York City, Olmsted first set foot on southern soil in Washington, D.C., still very much a slaveholding city embedded between two slaveholding states, Maryland and Virginia (see map, page 11). His first dispatch published in the New York Daily Times *became the first chapter of* The Cotton Kingdom. *After two full days in the nation's capital, Olmsted moved south into Virginia and wrote as extensively about what he observed there as he did about any other state until he arrived in*

Louisiana and Texas. The selections in this chapter that relate to Washington and Virginia provide a taste of the range of venues and topics Olmsted would cover in the rest of his commentary: urban life for slaves and free blacks; the dynamics of the slave trade, labor systems, racial and class relations, and other issues gleaned from conversation with native Virginians or his own observations; and descriptions of the rural landscape and agricultural practices. He based his commentary on the latter primarily on an extended visit to a single farm, a technique he would employ throughout this and subsequent trips.

Olmsted moved into North Carolina by way of the Great Dismal Swamp, which straddles the Virginia–North Carolina border. There he discovered an unusual use of slave labor in the lumber and turpentine industries, both unconventional and little recognized aspects of the southern economy and of slavery's application. Curiously, for a book titled The Cotton Kingdom, *there is relatively little mention of cotton in either this or the next chapter.*

Nor did Olmsted have much to say about Charleston as he moved into South Carolina. It seems odd that he would omit his descriptions of the city from this volume, given its central role not only in kicking off the secession crisis in December 1860 but also in bringing on the war, with the showdown over Fort Sumter having taken place even as he was putting this book together. He chose to keep his focus instead on the journey itself, specifically on the multiple means of transportation—from boat to train to stagecoach—required to get from Wilmington, North Carolina, to Charleston, and on his various observations of the slaves, slaveholders, and other interesting characters he met along the way. Included is his encounter with a free black North Carolinian and his son, who were struggling to sell the tobacco they had raised for South Carolina markets.

1. WASHINGTON, D.C.

Washington, Dec. 16th.—Visiting the market-place, early on Tuesday morning, I found myself in the midst of a throng of a very different character from any I have ever seen at the North. The majority of the people were negroes; and, taken as a whole, they appeared inferior in the expression of their face and less well-clothed than any collection of negroes I had ever seen before. All the negro characteristics were more clearly marked in each than they often are in any at the North. In their dress, language, manner, motions—all were distinguishable almost as much by their colour, from the white people who were distributed

among them, and engaged in the same occupations—chiefly selling
poultry, vegetables, and small country produce. The white men were,
generally, a mean-looking people, and but meanly dressed, but differently so from the negroes.

Most of the produce was in small, rickety carts, drawn by the smallest, ugliest, leanest lot of oxen and horses that I ever saw. There was
but one pair of horses in over a hundred that were tolerably good—a
remarkable proportion of them were maimed in some way. As for the
oxen, I do not believe New England and New York together could produce a single yoke as poor as the best of them.

The very trifling quantity of articles brought in and exposed for sale
by most of the market-people was noticeable; a peck of potatoes, three
bunches of carrots, two cabbages, six eggs and a chicken, would be
about the average stock in trade of all the dealers. Mr. F.[1] said that an old
negro woman once came to his door with a single large turkey, which
she pressed him to buy. Struck with her fatigued appearance, he made
some inquiries of her, and ascertained that she had been several days
coming from home, had travelled mainly on foot, and had brought the
turkey and nothing else with her. "Ole massa had to raise some money
somehow, and he not sell anyting else, so he tole me to catch the big
gobbler, and tote um down to Washington and see wot um would fotch."

Land may be purchased, within twenty miles of Washington, at from
ten to twenty dollars an acre. Most of it has been once in cultivation,
and, having been exhausted in raising tobacco, has been, for many
years, abandoned, and is now covered by a forest growth. Several New
Yorkers have lately speculated in the purchase of this sort of land, and,
as there is a good market for wood, and the soil, by the decay of leaves
upon it, and other natural causes, has been restored to moderate fertil-
ity, have made money by clearing and improving it. By deep ploughing
and liming, and the judicious use of manures, it is made quite productive; and, as equally cheap farms can hardly be found in any Free State,
in such proximity to as good markets for agricultural produce, there are
inducements for a considerable Northern immigration hither. It may
not be long before a majority of the inhabitants will be opposed to slavery, and desire its abolition within the District. Indeed, when Mr. [Wil-
liam H.] Seward proposed in the Senate to allow them to decide that
matter, the advocates of "popular sovereignty" made haste to vote down
the motion.

---

[1] In a common stylistic convention of nineteenth-century travel writing, authors often
identified those they encountered only by an initial in order to preserve their anonymity.

There are, already, more Irish and German labourers and servants than *slaves*; and, as many of the objections which free labourers have to going further south, do not operate in Washington, the proportion of white labourers is every year increasing. The majority of servants, however, are now *free* negroes, which class constitutes one-fifth of the entire population. The slaves are one-fifteenth, but are mostly owned out of the District, and hired annually to those who require their services. In the assessment of taxable property, for 1853, the slaves, owned or hired in the District, were valued at three hundred thousand dollars.

The coloured population voluntarily sustain several churches, schools, and mutual assistance and improvement societies, and there are evidently persons among them of no inconsiderable cultivation of mind.

2. TO RICHMOND BY TRAIN

Richmond, Dec. 16th [1852].—From Washington to Richmond, Virginia, by the regular great southern route—steamboat on the Potomac to Acquia Creek, and thence direct by rail. The boat makes 55 miles in 3½ hours, including two stoppages (12½ miles an hour); fare $2 (3.6 cents a mile). Flat rail; distance, 75 miles; time 5½ hours (13 miles an hour); farc, $3.50 (4⅔ cents a mile).

Not more than a third of the country, visible on this route, I should say, is cleared; the rest mainly a pine forest. Of the cleared land, not more than one quarter seems to have been lately in cultivation; the rest is grown over with briars and bushes, and a long, coarse grass of no value. But two crops seem to be grown upon the cultivated land—maize [corn] and wheat. The last is frequently sown in narrow beds and carefully surface-drained, and is looking remarkably well.

A good many old plantation mansions are to be seen; generally standing in a grove of white oaks, upon some hill-top. Most of them are constructed of wood, of two stories, painted white, and have, perhaps, a dozen rude-looking little log-cabins scattered around them, for the slaves. Now and then, there is one of more pretension, with a large porch or gallery in front, like that of Mount Vernon. These are generally in a heavy, compact style; less often, perhaps, than similar establishments at the North, in markedly bad, or vulgar taste, but seem in sad need of repairs.

The more common sort of habitations of the white people are either of logs or loosely boarded frames, a brick chimney running up outside, at one end: everything very slovenly and dirty about them. Swine, hounds, and black and white children, are commonly lying very promiscuously together on the ground about the doors.

I am struck with the close cohabitation and association of black and white—negro women are carrying black and white babies together in their arms; black and white children are playing together (not going to school together); black and white faces are constantly thrust together out of the doors, to see the train go by.

A fine-looking, well-dressed, and well-behaved coloured young man sat, together with a white man, on a seat in the cars. I suppose the man was his master; but he was much the less like a gentleman of the two. The railroad company advertise to take coloured people only in second-class trains; but servants seem to go with their masters everywhere. Once, to-day, seeing a lady entering the car at a way-station, with a family behind her, and that she was looking about to find a place where they could be seated together, I rose, and offered her my seat, which had several vacancies round it. She accepted it, without thanking me, and immediately installed in it a stout negro woman; took the adjoining seat herself, and seated the rest of her party before her. It consisted of a white girl, probably her daughter, and a bright and very pretty mulatto girl. They all talked and laughed together; and the girls munched confectionary out of the same paper, with a familiarity and closeness of intimacy that would have been noticed with astonishment, if not with manifest displeasure, in almost any chance company at the North. When the negro is definitely a slave, it would seem that the alleged natural antipathy of the white race to associate with him is lost.

I am surprised at the number of fine-looking mulattoes, or nearly white-coloured persons, that I see. The majority of those with whom I have come personally in contact are such. I fancy I see a peculiar expression among these—a contraction of the eyebrows and tightening of the lips—a spying, secretive, and counsel-keeping expression.

But the great mass, as they are seen at work, under overseers, in the fields, appear very dull, idiotic, and brute-like; and it requires an effort to appreciate that they are, very much more than the beasts they drive, our brethren—a part of ourselves. They are very ragged, and the women especially, who work in the field with the men, with no apparent distinction in their labour, disgustingly dirty. They seem to move very awkwardly, slowly, and undecidedly, and almost invariably stop their work while the train is passing.

One tannery and two or three saw-mills afforded the only indications I saw, in seventy-five miles of this old country—settled before any part of Massachusetts—of any industrial occupation other than corn and wheat culture, and fire-wood chopping. At Fredericksburg we passed through the streets of a rather busy, poorly-built town; but altogether, the country seen from the railroad, bore less signs of an active and prospering people than any I ever travelled through before, for an equal distance.

Richmond, at a glance from adjacent high ground, through a dull cloud of bituminous smoke, upon a lowering winter's day, has a very picturesque appearance, and I was reminded of the sensation produced by a similar *coup d'œil* [glimpse] of Edinburgh. It is somewhat similarly situated upon and among some considerable hills; but the moment it is examined at all in detail, there is but one spot, in the whole picture, upon which the eye is at all attracted to rest. This is the Capitol, a Grecian edifice, standing alone, and finely placed, on open and elevated ground, in the centre of the town. It was built soon after the Revolution, and the model was obtained by Mr. Jefferson, then Minister to France, from the Maison Carrée.[1]

A considerable part of the town, which contains a population of 28,000, is compactly and somewhat substantially built, but is without any pretensions to architectural merit, except in a few modern private mansions. The streets are not paved, and but few of them are provided with side walks other than of earth or gravel. The town is lighted with gas, and furnished with excellent water by an aqueduct.

[1] A well-preserved Roman temple located in Nîmes, in southern France. Jefferson designed the capitol in Richmond in 1788, making it the first public building in North America constructed in the Monumental Classical style.

3. BLACK RICHMOND

The greater part of the coloured people, on Sunday, seemed to be dressed in the cast-off fine clothes of the white people, received, I suppose, as presents, or purchased of the Jews, whose shops show that there must be considerable importation of such articles, probably from the North, as there is from England into Ireland. Indeed, the lowest class, especially among the younger, remind me much, by their dress, of the "lads" of Donnybrook; and when the funeral procession came to its destination, there was a scene precisely like that you may see every day in Sackville Street, Dublin, —a dozen boys in ragged clothes, originally made for tall men, and rather folded round their bodies than worn, striving who should hold the horses of the gentlemen when they dismounted to attend the interment of the body. Many, who had probably come in from the farms near the town, wore clothing of coarse gray "negro-cloth," that appeared as if made by contract, without regard to the size of the particular individual to whom it had been allotted, like penitentiary uniforms. A few had a better suit of coarse blue cloth, expressly made for them evidently, for "Sunday clothes."

Some were dressed with foppish extravagance, and many in the latest style of fashion. In what I suppose to be the fashionable streets, there were many more well-dressed and highly-dressed coloured people than white; and among this dark gentry the finest French cloths, embroidered waistcoats, patent-leather shoes, resplendent brooches, silk hats, kid gloves, and *eau de mille fleurs* [a type of cologne], were quite common. Nor was the fairer, or rather the softer sex, at all left in the shade of this splendour. Many of the coloured ladies were dressed not only expensively, but with good taste and effect, after the latest Parisian mode. . . .

There was no indication of their belonging to a subject race, except that they invariably gave the way to the white people they met. Once, when two of them, engaged in conversation and looking at each other, had not noticed his approach, I saw a Virginian gentleman lift his walking-stick and push a woman aside with it. In the evening I saw three rowdies, arm-in-arm, taking the whole of the sidewalk, hustle a black man off it, giving him a blow, as they passed, that sent him staggering into the middle of the street. As he recovered himself he began to call out to, and threaten them. Perhaps he saw me stop, and thought I should support him, as I was certainly inclined to: "Can't you find anything else to do than to be knockin' quiet people round! You jus' come back here, will you? Here, you! *don't care if you is white*. You jus' come back here, and I'll teach you how to behave—knockin' people round!—don't care if I does hab to go to der watch-house." They passed on without noticing him further, only laughing jeeringly—and he continued: "You come back here, and I'll make you laugh; you is jus' three white nigger cowards, dat's what *you* be."

I observe, in the newspapers, complaints of growing insolence and insubordination among the negroes, arising, it is thought, from too many privileges being permitted them by their masters, and from too merciful administration of the police laws with regard to them. Except in this instance, however, I have seen not the slightest evidence of any independent manliness on the part of the negroes towards the whites. As far as I have yet observed, they are treated very kindly and even generously as servants, but their manner to white people is invariably either sullen, jocose, or fawning.

The pronunciation and dialect of the negroes, here, is generally much more idiomatic and peculiar than with us. As I write, I hear a man shouting, slowly and deliberately, meaning to say *there*: "*Dah! dah!* DAH!"

Among the people you see in the streets, full half, I should think, are more or less of negro blood, and a very decent, civil people these seem, in general, to be; more so than the labouring class of whites, among which there are many very ruffianly-looking fellows. There is a considerable population of foreign origin, generally of the least valuable class; very dirty German Jews, especially, abound, and their characteristic shops (with their characteristic smells, quite as bad as in Cologne) are thickly set in the narrowest and meanest streets, which seem to be otherwise inhabited mainly by negroes.

Immense waggons, drawn by six mules each, the teamster always riding on the back of the near-wheeler [like a running board], are a characteristic feature of the streets. On the canal, a long, narrow, canoe-like boat, perhaps fifty feet long and six wide, and drawing but a foot or two of water, is nearly as common as the ordinary large boats, such as are used on our canals. They come out of some of the small, narrow, crooked streams, connected with the canals, in which a difficult navigation is effected by poling. They are loaded with tobacco, flour, and a great variety of raw country produce. The canal boatmen seem rude, insolent, and riotous, and every facility is evidently afforded them, at Richmond, for indulging their peculiar appetites and tastes. A great many low eating, and, I should think, drinking, shops are frequented chiefly by the negroes. Dancing and other amusements are carried on in these at night.

From reading the comments of Southern statesmen and newspapers on the crime and misery which sometimes result from the accumulation of poor and ignorant people, with no intelligent masters to take care of them, in our Northern towns, one might get the impression that Southern towns—especially those not demoralized by foreign commerce—were comparatively free from a low and licentious population. From what I have seen, however, I am led to think that there is at least as much vice, and of what we call rowdyism, in Richmond, as in any Northern town of its size.

4. VIRGINIA'S SLAVE TRADE

Richmond. —Yesterday morning, during a cold, sleety storm, against which I was struggling, with my umbrella, to the post-office, I met a comfortably-dressed negro leading three others by a rope; the first was a middle-aged man; the second a girl of, perhaps, twenty; and the last a boy, considerably younger. The arms of all three were secured before them with hand-cuffs, and the rope by which they were led passed from one to another; being made fast at each pair of hand-cuffs. They were thinly clad, the girl especially so, having only an old ragged handkerchief around her neck, over a common calico dress, and another handkerchief twisted around her head. They were dripping wet, and icicles were forming, at the time, on the awning bars.

The boy looked most dolefully, and the girl was turning around, with a very angry face, and shouting, "O pshaw! Shut up!"

"What are they?" said I, to a white man, who had also stopped, for a moment, to look at them. "What's he going to do with them?"

"Come in a canal boat, I reckon: sent down here to be sold.—That ar's a likely gal."

Our ways lay together, and I asked further explanation. He informed me that the negro-dealers had confidential servants always in attendance, on the arrival of the railroad trains and canal packets, to take any negroes that might have come consigned to them, and bring them to their marts. . . .

Near the post-office, opposite a large livery and sale stable, I turned into a short, broad street, in which were a number of establishments, the signs on which indicated that they were occupied by "Slave Dealers," and that "Slaves, for Sale or to Hire," were to be found within them. They were much like Intelligence Offices, being large rooms partly occupied by ranges of forms, on which sat a few comfortably and neatly clad negroes, who appeared perfectly cheerful, each grinning obsequiously, but with a manifest interest or anxiety, when I fixed my eye on them for a moment.

. . . I did not myself happen to witness, during fourteen months that I spent in the Slave States, any sale of negroes by auction. This must not be taken as an indication that negro auctions are not of frequent occurrence (I did not, so far as I now recollect, witness the sale of anything else, at auction, at the South). I saw negroes advertised to be sold at auction, very frequently.

5. VISIT TO A VIRGINIA FARM

This morning I visited a farm, situated on the bank of James River, near Richmond.

The labour upon it was entirely performed by slaves. I did not inquire their number, but I judged there were from twenty to forty. Their "quarters" lined the approach-road to the mansion, and were well-made and comfortable log cabins, about thirty feet long by twenty wide, and eight feet tall, with a high loft and shingle roof. Each divided in the middle, and having a brick chimney outside the wall at either end, was intended to be occupied by two families. There were square windows, closed by wooden ports, having a single pane of glass in the centre. The house-servants were neatly dressed, but the field-hands wore very coarse and ragged garments.

During the three hours, or more, in which I was in company with the proprietor, I do not think ten consecutive minutes passed uninterrupted by some of the slaves requiring his personal direction or assistance. He was even obliged, three times, to leave the dinner-table.

"You see," said he, smiling, as he came in the last time, "a farmer's life, in this country, is no sinecure [a position that provides an income but requires little or no work]." Then turning the conversation to slavery, he observed, in answer to a remark of mine, "I only wish your philanthropists would contrive some satisfactory plan to relieve us of it; the trouble and the responsibility of properly taking care of our negroes, you may judge, from what you see yourself here, is anything but enviable. But what can we do that is better? Our free negroes—and I believe it is the same at the North as it is here—are a miserable set of vagabonds, drunken, vicious, worse off, it is my honest opinion, than those who are retained in slavery. I am satisfied, too, that our slaves are better off, as they are, than the majority of your free labouring classes at the North."

I expressed my doubts.

"Well, they certainly are better off than the English agricultural labourers, or, I believe, those of any other Christian country. Free labour might be more profitable to us: I am inclined to think it would be. The slaves are excessively careless and wasteful, and, in various ways—which, without you lived among them, you could hardly be made to understand—subject us to very annoying losses.

"To make anything by farming, here, a man has got to live a hard life. You see how constantly I am called upon—and, often, it is about as bad at night as by day. Last night I did not sleep a wink till near morning; I am quite worn out with it, and my wife's health is failing. But I cannot rid myself of it."

I asked why he did not employ an overseer.

"Because I do not think it right to trust to such men as we have to use, if we use any, for overseers."

"Is the general character of overseers bad?"

"They are the curse of this country, sir; the worst men in the community. . . . But lately, I had another sort of fellow offer—a fellow like a dancing-master, with kid gloves, and wrist-bands turned up over his coat-sleeves, and all so nice, that I was almost ashamed to talk to him in my old coat and slouched hat. Half a bushel of recommendations he had with him, too. Well, he was not the man for me—not half the gentleman, with all his airs, that Ned here is"—(a black servant, who was bursting with suppressed laughter, behind his chair).

"Oh, they are interesting creatures, sir," he continued, "and, with all their faults, have many beautiful traits. I can't help being attached to them, and I am sure they love us." In his own case, at least, I did not doubt it; his manner towards them was paternal—familiar and kind; and they came to him like children who have been given some task, and constantly are wanting to be encouraged and guided, simply and confidently. At dinner, he frequently addressed the servant familiarly, and drew him into our conversation as if he were a family friend, better informed, on some local and domestic points, than himself.

6. DISCUSSION OF SLAVE SALES AND SLAVE LABOR

There were, in the train [to Petersburg], two first-class passenger cars, and two freight cars. The latter were occupied by about forty negroes, most of them belonging to traders, who were sending them to the cotton States to be sold. Such kind of evidence of activity in the slave trade of Virginia is to be seen every day; but particulars and statistics of it are not to be obtained by a stranger here. Most gentlemen of character seem to have a special disinclination to converse on the subject; and it is denied, with feeling, that slaves are often reared, as is supposed by the Abolitionists, with the intention of selling them to the traders. It appears to me evident, however, from the manner in which I hear the traffic spoken of incidentally, that the cash value of a slave for sale, above the cost of raising it from infancy to the age at which it commands the highest price, is generally considered among the surest elements of a planter's wealth. Such a nigger is worth such a price, and such another is too old to learn to pick cotton, and such another will bring so much, when it has grown a little more, I have frequently heard people say, in the street, or the public-houses. That a slave woman is commonly esteemed least for her working qualities, most for those qualities which give value to a brood-mare is, also, constantly made apparent.

By comparing the average decennial ratio [calculated every ten years through the U.S. Census] of slave increase in all the States with the difference in the number of the actual slave-population of the slave-breeding States, as ascertained by the Census, it is apparent that the number of slaves exported to the cotton States is considerably more than twenty thousand a year.

While calling on a gentleman occupying an honourable official position at Richmond, I noticed upon his table a copy of Professor Johnson's *Agricultural Tour in the United States*. Referring to a paragraph in it, where some statistics of the value of the slaves raised and annually exported from Virginia were given, I asked if he knew how these had been obtained, and whether they were authentic. "No," he replied, "I don't know anything about it; but if they are anything unfavourable to the institution of slavery, you may be sure they are false." This is but an illustration, in extreme, of the manner in which I find a desire to obtain more correct but *definite* information, on the subject of slavery, is usually met, by gentlemen otherwise of enlarged mind and generous qualities.

A gentleman, who was a member of the "Union Safety Committee" of New York, during the excitement which attended the discussion of the Fugitive Slave Act of 1850, told me that, as he was passing through Virginia this winter, a man entered the car in which he was seated, leading in a negro girl, whose manner and expression of face indicated dread and grief. Thinking she was a criminal, he asked the man what she had done.

"Done? Nothing."

"What are you going to do with her?"

"I'm taking her down to Richmond, to be sold."

"Does she belong to you?"

"No; she belongs to——; he raised her."

"Why does he sell her—has she done anything wrong?"

"Done anything? No: she's no fault, I reckon."

"Then, what does he want to sell her for?"

"Sell her for! Why shouldn't he sell her? He sells one or two every year; wants the money for 'em, I reckon."

The irritated tone and severe stare with which this was said, my friend took as a caution not to pursue his investigation.

A gentleman with whom I was conversing on the subject of the cost of slave labour, in answer to an inquiry—What proportion of all the stock of slaves of an old plantation might be reckoned upon to do full work?—answered, that he owned ninety-six negroes; of these, only thirty-five were field-hands, the rest being either too young or too old for hard work. He reckoned his whole force as only equal to twenty-one strong men, or "*prime* field-hands." But this proportion was somewhat smaller than usual, he added, "because his women were uncommonly good breeders; he did not suppose there was a lot of women anywhere that bred faster than his; he never heard of babies coming so fast as they did on his plantation; it was perfectly surprising; and every one of them, in his estimation, was worth two hundred dollars, as negroes were selling now, the moment it drew breath."

I asked what he thought might be the usual proportion of workers to slaves, supported on plantations, throughout the South. On the large cotton and sugar plantations of the more Southern States, it was very high, he replied; because their hands were nearly all bought and *picked for work*; he supposed, on these, it would be about one-half; but, on any old plantation, where the stock of slaves had been an inheritance, and none had been bought or sold, he thought the working force would rarely be more than one-third, at most, of the whole number.

7. CONVERSATION WITH A WHITE TOBACCO FARMER

A little beyond the fork, there was a large, gray, old house, with a grove of tall poplars before it; a respectable, country-gentleman-of-the-old-school look it had. . . .

. . . Beyond the house, a gate opened on the road, and out of this was just then coming a black man.

I inquired of him if there was a house, near by, at which I could get accommodation for the night. Reckoned his master'd take me in, if I'd ask him. Where was his master? In the house: I could go right in here (at a place where a panel of the paling [fence] had fallen over) and see him if I wanted to. I asked him to hold my horse, and went in.

It was a simple two-story house, very much like those built by the wealthier class of people in New England villages, from fifty to a hundred years ago, except that the chimneys were carried up outside the walls. There was a porch at the front door, and a small wing at one end, in the rear: from this wing to the other end extended a broad gallery.

A dog had been barking at me after I had dismounted; and just as I reached the steps of the gallery, a vigorous, middle-aged man, with a rather sullen and suspicious expression of face, came out without any coat on, to see what had excited him.

Doubting if he were the master of the house, I told him that I had come in to inquire if it would be convenient to allow me to spend the night with them. He asked where I came from, whither I was going, and various other questions, until I had given him an epitome of my day's wanderings and adventures; at the conclusion of which he walked to the end of the gallery to look at my horse; then, without giving me any answer, but muttering indistinctly something about servants, walked into the house, shutting the door behind him!

Well, thought I, this is not overwhelmingly hospitable. What can it mean?

While I was considering whether he expected me to go without any further talk—his curiosity being, I judged, satisfied—he came out again, and said, "Reckon you can stay, sir, if you'll take what we'll give you." (The good man had been in to consult his wife.) I replied that I would do so thankfully, and hoped they would not give themselves any unnecessary trouble, or alter their usual family arrangements. I was then invited to come in, but I preferred to see my horse taken care of first. My host called for "Sam," two or three times, and then said he reckoned all his "people" had gone off, and he would attend to my horse himself. I offered to assist him, and we walked out to the gate, where the negro, not being inclined to wait for my return, had left Jane fastened to a post. Our host conducted us to an old square log-cabin which had formerly been used for curing tobacco, there being no room for Jane, he said, in the stables proper.

The floor of the tobacco-house was covered with lumber, old ploughs, scythes and cradles, a part of which had to be removed to make room for the filly to stand. She was then induced, with some difficulty, to enter it through a low, square doorway; saddle and bridle were removed, and she was fastened in a corner by a piece of old plough-line. We then went to a fodder-stack, and pulled out from it several small bundles of maize leaves. Additional feed and water were promised when "some of the niggers" came in; and, after righting up an old door that had fallen from one hinge, and setting a rail against it to keep it in its place, we returned to the house.

My host (whom I will call Mr. Newman) observed that his buildings and fences were a good deal out of order. He had owned the place but a few years, and had not had time to make much improvement about the house yet.

Entering the mansion, he took me to a large room on the first floor, gave me a chair, went out and soon returned (now wearing a coat) with two negro girls, one bringing wood and the other some flaming brands. A fire was made with a great deal of trouble, scolding of the girls, bringing in more brands, and blowing with the mouth. When the room had been suffocatingly filled with smoke, and at length a strong bright blaze swept steadily up the chimney, Mr. Newman again went out with the girls, and I was left alone for nearly an hour. . . .

. . . The house had evidently been built for a family of some wealth, and, after having been deserted by them, had been bought at a bargain by the present resident, who either had not the capital or the inclination to furnish and occupy it appropriately.

When my entertainer called again, he merely opened the door and said, "Come! get something to eat!" I followed him out into the gallery, and thence through a door at its end into a room in the wing—a family room, and a very comfortable homely room. A bountifully spread supper-table stood in the centre, at which was sitting a very neat, pretty little woman, of as silent habits as her husband, but neither bashful nor morose. A very nice little girl sat at her right side, and a peevish, ill-behaved, whining glutton of a boy at her left. . . .

The two negro girls waited at table, and a negro boy was in the room, who, when I asked for a glass of water, was sent to get it. An old negro woman also frequently came in from the kitchen, with hot biscuit and corn-cake. There was fried fowl, and fried bacon and eggs, and cold ham; there were preserved peaches, and preserved quinces and grapes; there was hot wheaten biscuit, and hot short-cake, and hot corn-cake, and hot griddle cakes, soaked in butter; there was coffee, and there was milk, sour or sweet, whichever I preferred to drink. I really ate more than I wanted, and extolled the corn-cake and the peach preserve. . . .

I . . . went to the sitting-room, where I found Miss Martha Ann and her kitten; I was having a good time with her, when her father [Mr. Newman] came in and told her she was "troubling the gentleman." I denied it, and he took a seat by the fire with us, and I soon succeeded in drawing him into a conversation on farming, and the differences in our methods of work at the North and those he was accustomed to.

I learned that there were no white labouring men here who hired themselves out by the month. The poor white people that had to labour for their living, never would work steadily at any employment. "They generally followed boating"—hiring as hands on the bateaus that navigate the small streams and canals, but never for a longer term at once than a single trip of a boat, whether that might be long or short. At the end of the trip they were paid by the day. Their wages were from fifty cents to a dollar, varying with the demand and individual capacities. They hardly ever worked on farms except in harvest, when they usually received a dollar a day, sometimes more. In harvest-time, most of the rural mechanics closed their shops and hired out to the farmers at a dollar a day, which would indicate that their ordinary earnings are considerably less than this. At other than harvest-time, the poor white people, who had no trade, would sometimes work for the farmers by the job; not often any regular agricultural labour, but at getting rails or shingles, or clearing land.

He did not know that they were particular about working with negroes, but no white man would ever do certain kinds of work (such as taking care of cattle, or getting water or wood to be used in the house); and if you should ask a white man you had hired, to do such things, he would get mad and tell you he wasn't a nigger. Poor white girls never hired out to do servants' work, but they would come and help another white woman about her sewing and quilting, and take wages for it. But these girls were not very respectable generally, and it was not agreeable to have them in your house, though there were some very respectable ladies that would go out to sew. Farmers depended almost entirely upon their negroes; it was only when they were hard pushed by their crops, that they ever got white hands to help them.

Negroes had commanded such high wages lately, to work on railroads and in tobacco-factories, that farmers were tempted to hire out too many of their people, and to undertake to do too much work with those they retained; and thus they were often driven to employ white men, and to give them very high wages by the day, when they found themselves getting much behind-hand with their crops. He had been driven very hard in this way this last season; he had been so unfortunate as to lose one of his best women, who died in child-bed just before harvest. The loss of the woman and her child, for the child had died also, just at that time, came very hard upon him. He would not have taken a thousand dollars of any man's money for them. He had had to hire white men to help him, but they were poor sticks, and would be half the time drunk, and you never know what to depend upon with them. One fellow that he had hired, who had agreed to work for him all through harvest, got him to pay him some wages in advance (he said it was to buy him some clothes with, so that he could go to meeting on Sunday, at the Court House), and went off the next day, right in the middle of harvest, and he had never seen him since. He had heard of him—he was on a boat—but he didn't reckon he should ever get his money again.

Of course, he did not see how white labourers were ever going to come into competition with negroes here, at all. You never could depend on white men, and you couldn't *drive* them any; they wouldn't stand it. Slaves were the only reliable labourers—you could command them and make them do what was right.

8. SLAVES' WORK ETHIC

A well-informed capitalist and slave-holder remarked, that negroes could not be employed in cotton factories. I said that I understood they were so in Charleston, and some other places at the South.

"It may be so, yet," he answered, "but they will have to give it up."

The reason was, he said, that the negro could never be trained to exercise judgment; he cannot be made to use his mind; he always depends on machinery doing its own work, and cannot be made to watch it. He neglects it until something is broken or there is great waste. "We have tried rewards and punishments, but it makes no difference. It's his nature and you cannot change it. All men are indolent and have a disinclination to labour, but this is a great deal stronger in the African race than in any other. In working niggers, we must always calculate that they will not labour at all except to avoid punishment, and they will never do more than just enough to save themselves from being punished, and no amount of punishment will prevent their working carelessly and indifferently. It always seems on the plantation as if they took pains to break all the tools and spoil all the cattle that they possibly can, even when they know they'll be directly punished for it."

As to rewards, he said, "They only want to support life: they will not work for anything more; and in this country it would be hard to prevent their getting that." I thought this opinion of the power of rewards was not exactly confirmed by the narrative we had just heard, but I said nothing. "If you could move," he continued, "all the white people from the whole seaboard district of Virginia and give it up to the negroes that are on it now, just leave them to themselves, in ten years' time there would not be an acre of land cultivated, and nothing would be produced, except what grew spontaneously."

9. SLAVE LUMBERMEN IN THE GREAT DISMAL SWAMP

Jan. 18th. —The "Great Dismal Swamp," together with the smaller "Dismals" (for so the term is used here), of the same character, along the North Carolina coast, have hitherto been of considerable commercial importance as furnishing a large amount of lumber, and especially of shingles for our Northern use, as well as for exportation. The district from which this commerce proceeds is all a vast quagmire, the soil being entirely composed of decayed vegetable fibre, saturated and surcharged with water; yielding or *quaking* on the surface to the tread of a man, and a large part of it, during most of the year, half inundated with standing pools. . . .

The labour in the swamp is almost entirely done by slaves; and the way in which they are managed is interesting and instructive. They are mostly hired by their employers at a rent, perhaps of one hundred dollars a year for each, paid to their owners. They spend one or two months of the winter—when it is too wet to work in the swamp—at the residence of their master. At this period little or no work is required of them; their time is their own, and if they can get any employment, they will generally keep for themselves what they are paid for it. When it is sufficiently dry—usually early in February—they go into the swamp in gangs, each gang under a white overseer. Before leaving, they are all examined and registered at the Court House; and "passes," good for a year, are given them, in which their features and the marks upon their persons are minutely described. Each man is furnished with a quantity of provisions and clothing, of which, as well as of all that he afterwards draws from the stock in the hands of the overseer, an exact account is kept.

Arrived at their destination, a rude camp is made; huts of logs, poles, shingles, and boughs being built, usually, upon some places where shingles have been worked before, and in which the shavings have accumulated in small hillocks upon the soft surface of the ground.

The slave lumberman then lives measurably as a free man; hunts, fishes, eats, drinks, smokes and sleeps, plays and works, each when and as much as he pleases. It is only required of him that he shall have made, after half a year has passed, such a quantity of shingles as shall be worth to his master so much money as is paid to his owner for his services, and shall refund the value of the clothing and provisions he has required.

No "driving" at his work is attempted or needed. No force is used to overcome the indolence peculiar to the negro. The overseer merely takes a daily account of the number of shingles each man adds to the general stock, and employs another set of hands, with mules, to draw them to a point from which they can be shipped, and where they are, from time to time, called for by a schooner.

At the end of five months the gang returns to dry land, and a statement of account from the overseer's book is drawn up, something like the following:

SAM BO TO JOHN DOE, DR.

Feb. 1. To clothing (outfit).	$ 5 00
Mar. 10. To clothing, as per overseer's account.	2 25
Feb. 1. To bacon and meal (outfit).	19 00
July 1. To stores drawn in swamp, as per overseer's account.	4 75
July 1. To half-yearly hire, paid his owner.	50 00
	$ 81 00

PER CONTRA[CT], CR[EDIT]

July 1. By 10,000 shingles, as per overseer's account, 10 c[ents each]	100 00
Balance due Sambo	$ 19 00

which is immediately paid him, and of which, together with the proceeds of sale of peltry [animal skins] which he has got while in the swamp, he is always allowed to make use as his own. No liquor is sold or served to the negroes in the swamp, and, as their first want when they come out of it is an excitement, most of their money goes to the grog-shops.

After a short vacation, the whole gang is taken in the schooner to spend another five months in the swamp as before. If they are good hands and work steadily, they will commonly be hired again, and so continuing, will spend most of their lives at it. They almost invariably have excellent health, as have also the white men engaged in the business. They all consider the water of the "Dismals" to have a medicinal virtue, and quite probably it is a mild tonic. It is greenish in colour, and I thought I detected a slightly resinous taste upon first drinking it. Upon entering the swamp also, an agreeable resinous odour, resembling that of a hemlock forest, was perceptible.

The negroes working in the swamp were more sprightly and straightforward in their manner and conversation than any field-hand plantation negroes that I saw at the South; two or three of their employers with whom I conversed spoke well of them, as compared with other slaves, and made no complaints of "rascality" or laziness.

One of those gentlemen told me of a remarkable case of providence and good sense in a negro that he had employed in the swamp for many years. He was so trustworthy, that he had once let him go to New York as cook of a lumber schooner, when he could, if he had chosen to remain there, have easily escaped from slavery.

Knowing that he must have accumulated considerable money, his employer suggested to him that he might *buy* his freedom, and he immediately determined to do so. But when, on applying to his owner, he was asked $500 for himself, a price which, considering he was an elderly man, he thought too much, he declined the bargain; shortly afterwards, however, he came to his employer again, and said that although he thought his owner was mean to set so high a price upon him, he had been thinking that if he was to be an old man he would rather be his own master, and if he did not live long, his money would not be of any use to him at any rate, and so he had concluded he would make the purchase.

He did so, and upon collecting the various sums that he had loaned to white people in the vicinity, he was found to have several hundred dollars more than was necessary. With the surplus, he paid for his passage to Liberia,[1] and bought a handsome outfit. When he was about to leave, my informant had made him a present, and, in thanking him for it, the free man had said that the first thing he should do, on reaching Liberia, would be to learn to write, and, as soon as he could, he would write to him how he liked the country: he had been gone yet scarce a year, and had not been heard from.

[1] In 1821, officials of the American Colonization Society purchased territory in West Africa for the purpose of sending newly freed African American slaves there for settlement. Named Liberia, the colony was never more than a partial success, although by 1860 more than twelve thousand former slaves had chosen to settle there. Liberia was declared an independent republic in 1847.

10. NORTH CAROLINA'S TURPENTINE INDUSTRY

Fayetteville. — The negroes employed in the turpentine business, to which during the last week I have been giving some examination, seem to me to be unusually intelligent and cheerful, decidedly more so than most of the white people inhabiting the turpentine forest. Among the latter there is a large number, I should think a majority, of entirely uneducated, poverty-stricken vagabonds. I mean by vagabonds, simply, people without habitual, definite occupation or reliable means of livelihood. They are poor, having almost no property but their own bodies; and the use of these, that is, their labour, they are not accustomed to hire out statedly and regularly, so as to obtain capital by wages, but only occasionally by the day or job, when driven to it by necessity. A family of these people will commonly hire, or "squat" and build, a little log cabin, so made that it is only a shelter from rain, the sides not being chinked, and having no more furniture or pretension to comfort than is commonly provided a criminal in the cell of a prison. They will cultivate a little corn, and possibly a few roods [rows] of potatoes, cow-peas, and coleworts. They will own a few swine, that find their living in the forest; and pretty certainly, also, a rifle and dogs; and the men, ostensibly, occupy most of their time in hunting. I am, mainly, repeating the statements of one of the turpentine distillers, but it was confirmed by others, and by my own observation, so far as it went.

A gentleman of Fayetteville told me that he had, several times, appraised, under oath, the whole household property of families of this class at less than $20. If they have need of money to purchase clothing, etc., they obtain it by selling their game or meal. If they have none of this to spare, or an insufficiency, they will work for a neighbouring farmer for a few days, and they usually get for their labour fifty cents a day. . . . The farmers and distillers say, that that they do not like to employ them, because they cannot be relied upon to finish what they undertake, or to work according to directions; and because, being white men, they cannot "drive" them. That is to say, their labour is even more inefficient and unmanageable than that of slaves. . . .

The majority of what I have termed turpentine-farmers—meaning the small proprietors of the long-leafed pine forest land—are people but a grade superior, in character or condition, to these vagabonds. They have habitations more like houses—log-cabins, commonly, sometimes chinked, oftener not—without windows of glass, but with a few pieces of substantial old-fashioned heir-loom furniture; a vegetable garden, in which, however, you will find no vegetable but what they call "collards" (colewort) for "greens"; fewer dogs, more swine, and larger clearings for maize, but no better crops than the poorer class. Their property is, nevertheless, often of considerable money value, consisting mainly of negroes, who, associating intimately with their masters, are of superior intelligence to the slaves of the wealthier classes.

11. NORTH CAROLINA'S SLAVE ECONOMY AND BACKWARD CULTURE

North Carolina has a proverbial reputation for the ignorance and torpidity of her people; being, in this respect, at the head of the Slave States. I do not find the reason of this in any innate quality of the popular mind; but, rather, in the circumstances under which it finds its development. Owing to the general poverty of the soil in the eastern part of the State, and to the almost exclusive employment of slave labour on the soils productive of cotton; owing, also, to the difficulty and expense of reaching market with bulky produce from the interior and western districts, population and wealth are more divided than in the other Atlantic States; industry is almost entirely rural, and there is but little communication or concert of action among the small and scattered proprietors of capital. For the same reason, the advantages of education are more difficult to be enjoyed, the distance at which families reside apart preventing children from coming together in such numbers as to give remunerative employment to a teacher. The teachers are, generally, totally unfitted for their business; young men, as a clergyman informed me, themselves not only unadvanced beyond the lowest knowledge of the elements of primary school learning, but often coarse, vulgar, and profane in their language and behaviour, who take up teaching as a temporary business, to supply the demand of a neighbourhood of people as ignorant and uncultivated as themselves.

. . .

But the aspect of North Carolina with regard to slavery, is, in some respects, less lamentable than that of Virginia. There is not only less bigotry upon the subject, and more freedom of conversation, but I saw here, in the institution, more of patriarchal character than in any other State. The slave more frequently appears as a family servant—a member of his master's family, interested with him in his fortune, good or bad. This is a result of the less concentration of wealth in families or individuals, occasioned by the circumstances I have described. Slavery thus loses much of its inhumanity. It is still questionable, however, if, as the subject race approaches civilization, the dominant race is not proportionately detained in its onward progress. One is forced often to question, too, in viewing slavery in this aspect, whether humanity and the accumulation of wealth, the prosperity of the master, and the happiness and improvement of the subject, are not in some degree incompatible.

These later observations are made after having twice again passed through the State, once in a leisurely way on horseback. In some of the western and northern central parts of the State, there is much more enterprise, thrift, and comfort than in the eastern part, where I had my first impressions.

12. FROM WILMINGTON TO CHARLESTON

We reached Wilmington [N.C.], the port at the mouth of the river, at half-past nine. Taking a carriage, I was driven first to one hotel and afterwards to another. They were both so crowded with guests, and excessive business duties so prevented the clerks from being tolerably civil to me, that I feared if I remained in either of them I should have another Norfolk experience [a previous miserable stay in a poorly run hotel]. While I was endeavouring to ascertain if there was a third public-house, in which I might, perhaps, obtain a private room, my eye fell upon an advertisement of a new railroad line of passage to Charleston. A boat, to take passengers to the railroad, was to start every night, from Wilmington, at ten o'clock. It was already something past ten; but being pretty sure that she would not get off punctually, and having a strong resisting impulse to being packed away in a close room, with any chance stranger the clerk of the house might choose to couple me with, I shouldered my baggage and ran for the wharves. At half-past ten I was looking at Wilmington over the stern of another little wheel-barrow-steamboat, pushing back up the river. When or how I was to be taken to Charleston, I had not yet been able to ascertain. The captain assured me it was all right, and demanded twenty dollars. Being in his power I gave it to him, and received in return a pocketful of tickets, guaranteeing the bearer passage from place to place; of not one of which places had I ever heard before, except Charleston.

The cabin was small, dirty, crowded, close, and smoky. Finding a warm spot in the deck, over the furnace, and to leeward of the chimney, I pillowed myself on my luggage and went to sleep.

The ringing of the boat's bell awoke me, after no great lapse of time, and I found we were in a small creek, heading southward. Presently we reached a wharf, near which stood a locomotive and train. A long, narrow plank having been run out, half a dozen white men, including myself, went on shore. Then followed as many negroes, who appeared to be a recent purchase of their owner. Owing, probably, to an unusually low tide, there was a steep ascent from the boat to the wharf, and I was amused to see the anxiety of this gentleman for the safe landing of his property, and especially to hear him curse them for their carelessness, as if their lives were of much greater value to him than to themselves. One was a woman. All carried over their shoulders some little baggage, probably all their personal effects, slung in a blanket; and one had a dog, whose safe landing caused him nearly as much anxiety as his own did *his* owner.

"Gib me da dog, now," said the dog's owner, standing half way up the plank.

"Damn the dog," said the negro's owner; "give me your hand up here. Let go of the dog; d'ye hear! Let him take care of himself."

But the negro hugged the dog, and brought him safely on shore.

After a short delay the train started: the single passenger car was a fine one (made at Wilmington, Delaware), and just sufficiently warmed. I should have slept again if it had not been that two of the six inmates were drunk—one of them uproariously.

Passing through long stretches of cypress swamps, with occasional intervals of either pine-barrens, or clear water ponds, in about two hours we came, in the midst of the woods, to the end of the rails. In the vicinity could be seen a small tent, a shanty of loose boards, and a large, subdued fire, around which, upon the ground, a considerable number of men were stretched out asleep. This was the camp of the hands engaged in laying the rails, and who were thus daily extending the distance which the locomotive could run.

The conductor told me that there was here a break of about eighty miles in the rail, over which I should be transferred by a stage-coach, which would come as soon as possible after the driver knew that the train had arrived. To inform him of this, the locomotive trumpeted loud and long.

The negro property, which had been brought up in a freight car, was immediately let out on the stoppage of the train. As it stepped on to the platform, the owner asked, "Are you all here?"

"Yes, massa, we is all heah," answered one. "Do dysef no harm, for we's all heah," added another, in an undertone.

The negroes immediately gathered some wood, and taking a brand from the railroad hands, made a fire for themselves; then, all but the woman, opening their bundles, wrapped themselves in their blankets and went to sleep. The woman, bare-headed, and very inadequately clothed as she was, stood for a long time alone, erect and statue-like, her head bowed, gazing in the fire. She had taken no part in the light chat of the others, and had given them no assistance in making the fire. Her dress too was not the usual plantation apparel. It was all sadly suggestive.

13. NORTHERN HAY VS. SOUTHERN COTTON

The principal other freight of the train was one hundred and twenty bales of Northern hay. It belonged, as the conductor told me, to a planter who lived some twenty miles beyond here, and who had bought it in Wilmington at a dollar and a half a hundred weight, to feed his mules.

Including the steamboat and railroad freight, and all the labour of getting it to his stables, its entire cost to him would not be much less than two dollars a hundred, or at least four times as much as it would have cost to raise and make it in the interior of New York or New England. There are not only several forage crops which can be raised in South Carolina, that cannot be grown on account of the severity of the winter in the Free States, but, on a farm near Fayetteville, a few days before, I had seen a crop of natural grass growing in half-cultivated land, dead upon the ground; which, I think, would have made, if it had been cut and well treated in the summer, three tons of hay to the acre. The owner of the land said that there was no better hay than it would have made, but he hadn't had time to attend to it. He had as much as his hands could do of other work at the period of the year when it should have been made.

Probably the case was similar with the planter who had bought this Northern hay at a price four times that which it would have cost a Northern farmer to make it. He had preferred to employ his slaves at other business.

The inference must be, either that there was most improbably-foolish, bad management, or that the slaves were more profitably employed in cultivating cotton, than they could have been in cultivating maize, or other forage crops.

I put the case, some days afterwards, to an English merchant, who had had good opportunities, and made it a part of his business to study such matters.

"I have no doubt," said he, "that if hay cannot be obtained here, other valuable forage can, with less labour than anywhere at the North; and all the Southern agricultural journals sustain this opinion, and declare it to be purely bad management that neglects these crops, and devotes labour to cotton, so exclusively. Probably, it is so—at the present cost of forage. Nevertheless, the fact is also true, as the planters assert, that they cannot afford to apply their labour to anything else but cotton. And yet, they complain that the price of cotton is so low that there is no profit in growing it, which is evidently false. You see that they prefer buying hay to raising it at, to say the least, three times what it costs your Northern farmers to raise it. Of course, if cotton could be grown in New York and Ohio, it could be afforded at one-third the cost it is here—say at three cents per pound. And that is my solution of the slavery question. Bring cotton down to three cents a pound, and there would be more abolitionists in South Carolina than in Massachusetts. If that can be brought about, in any way—and it is not impossible that we may live to see it, as our railways are extended in India, and the French enlarge their free-labour plantations in Algiers—there will be an end of slavery."

14. CONVERSATION WITH A FREE BLACK TOBACCO FARMER

[*Near Marion, S.C.*]—While we were changing [the horses pulling the stagecoach] at a house near a crossing of roads, strolling off in the woods for a short distance, I came upon two small white-topped waggons, each with a pair of horses feeding at its pole; near them was a dull camp fire, with a bake-kettle and coffee-pot, some blankets and a chest upon the ground, and an old negro sitting with his head bowed down over a meal sack, while a negro boy was combing his wool with a common horse-card, "Good evening, uncle," said I, approaching them. "Good evening, sar," he answered, without looking up.

"Where are you going?"

"Well, we ain't gwine nower, master; we's peddlin' tobacco roun."

"Where did you come from?"

"From Rockingham County, Norf Ca'lina, master."

"How long have you been coming from there?"

"'Twill be seven weeks, to-morrow, sar, sin we leff home."

"Have you most sold out?"

"We had a hundred and seventy-five boxes in both waggons, and we's sold all but sixty. Want to buy some tobacco, master?" (Looking up.)

"No, thank you; I am only waiting here, while the coach changes. How much tobacco is there in a box?"

"Seventy-five pound."

"Are these the boxes?"

"No, them is our provision boxes, master. Show de genman some of der tobacco, dah." (To the boy.)

A couple of negroes here passed along near us; the old man hailed them:

"Ho dah, boys! Doan you want to buy some backey?"

"No." (Decidedly.)

"Well, I'm sorry for it." (Reproachfully.)

"Are you bound homeward, now?" I asked.

"No, master; wish me was; got to sell all our backey fuss; you don't want none, master, does you? Doan you tink it pretty fair tobacco, sar? Juss try it: it's right sweet, reckon you'll find."

"I don't wish any, thank you; I never use it. Is your master with you?"

"No, sar; he's gone across to Marion, to-day."

"Do you like to be travelling about, in this way?"

"Yes, master; I likes it very well."

"Better than staying at home, eh?"

"Well, I likes my country better dan dis; must say dat, master; likes my country better dan dis. I'se a free niggar in my country, master."

"Oh, you are a free man, are you! North Carolina is a better country than this, for free men, I suppose."

"Yes, master, I likes my country de best; I gets five dollar a month for dat boy." (Hastily, to change the subject.)

"He is your son, is he?"

"Yes, sar; he drives dat waggon, I drives dis; and I haant seen him fore, master, for six weeks, till dis mornin'."

"How were you separated?"

"We separated six weeks ago, sar, and we agreed to meet here, last night. We didn', dough, till dis mornin'."

The old man's tone softened, and he regarded his son with earnestness.

"'Pears, dough, we was bofe heah, last night; but I couldn't find um till dis mornin'. Dis mornin' some niggars tole me dar war a niggar camped off yander in de wood; and I knew 'twas him, and I went an' found him right off."

"And what wages do you get for yourself?"

"Ten dollars a month, master."

"That's pretty good wages."

"Yes, master, any niggar can get good wages if he's a mind to be industrious, no matter wedder he's slave or free."

"So you don't like this country as well as North Carolina?"

"No, master. Fac is, master, 'pears like wite folks doan' ginerally like niggars in dis country; day doan' ginerally talk so to niggars like as do in my country; de niggars ain't so happy heah; 'pears like de wite folks was kind o' different, somehow. I doan' like dis country so well; my country suits me very well."

"Well, I've been thinking, myself, the niggers did not look so well here as they did in North Carolina and Virginia; they are not so well clothed, and they don't appear so bright as they do there."

"Well, master, Sundays dey is mighty well clothed, dis country; 'pears like dere an't nobody looks better Sundays dan dey do. But Lord! workin' days, seems like dey haden no close dey could keep on 'um at all, master. Dey is a'mos' naked, wen deys at work, some on 'em. Why, master, up in our country, de wite folks—why, some on 'em has ten or twelve niggars; dey doan' hev no real big plantation, like day has heah, but some on 'em has ten or twelve niggars, may be, and dey juss lives and talks along wid 'em; and dey treats 'um most as if dem was dar own chile. Dey doan' keep no niggars dey can't treat so; dey won't keep 'em, won't be bodered wid 'em. If dey gets a niggar and he doan behave himself, dey won't keep him; dey juss tell him, sar, he must look up anudder master, and if he doan' find hisself one, I tell 'ou, when de trader cum along, dey sells him, and he totes him away. Dey allers sell off all de bad niggars out of our country; dat's de way all de bad niggar and all dem no-account niggar keep a cumin' down heah; dat's de way on't master."

"Yes, that's the way of it, I suppose; these big plantations are not just the best thing for niggers, I see that plainly."

Chapter 2

Georgia and Alabama

Olmsted traveled by boat from Charleston to Savannah on January 27, 1853, and spent the next month and a half moving through Georgia and Alabama (see map, page 11). The selections here include the first of his comprehensive descriptions of a plantation operation, this one a rice plantation along the coast just south of Savannah. (He provided equally in-depth coverage of sugar and cotton plantations, samples of which appear later in this volume.) The value of this coverage lies in how fully Olmsted described all he observed on these visits. He was as attentive to slave life and living quarters as he was to the master's home, furnishings, and lifestyle. He was a close observer of the agricultural scene as well, making note of techniques and processes, as well as the multifaceted divisions of labor—from slaves to overseers to drivers (or "watchmen," as referred to in Selection 17)—all the while attuned to the social hierarchy reflected by these work assignments and levels of authority. Notable, too, is Olmsted's description of a church service—one of several points in his chronicles in which he reveals a real interest in the role of religion in a slaveholding society.

15. TRAVELING THROUGH COASTAL GEORGIA

Plantation, February [1853].—I left [Savannah] yesterday morning, on horseback, with a letter in my pocket to Mr. X.,[1] under whose roof I am now writing. The weather was fine, and, indeed, since I left Virginia, the weather for out-of-door purposes has been as fine as can be imagined.

---

[1] Historians have identified Mr. X as the Georgia rice planter Richard J. Arnold, who referred to Olmsted's visit in his own diary. He is the subject of a full biography by Charles Hoffman and Tess Hoffman (see Selected Bibliography).

The exercise of walking or of riding warms one, at any time between sunrise and sunset, sufficiently to allow an overcoat to be dispensed with, while the air is yet brisk and stimulating. The public-houses are overcrowded with Northerners, who congratulate themselves on having escaped from the severe cold, of which they hear from home. . . .

As the number of Northerners, and especially of invalids, who come hither in winter, is every year increasing, more comfortable accommodations along the line of travel must soon be provided; if not by native, then by Northern enterprise. Some of the hotels in Florida, indeed, are already, I understand, under the management of Northerners; and this winter, cooks and waiters have been procured for them from the North. I observe, also, that one of them advertises that meats and vegetables are received by every steamer from New York.

Whenever comfortable quarters, and means of conveyance are extensively provided, at not immoderately great expense, there must be a great migration here every winter. The climate and the scenery, as well as the society of the more wealthy planters' families, are attractive, not to invalids alone, but even more to men and women who are able to enjoy invigorating recreations. Nowhere in the world could a man, with a sound body and a quiet conscience, live more pleasantly, at least as a guest, it seems to me, than here where I am. . . .

But I must tell how I got here, and what I saw by the way.

A narrow belt of cleared land—"vacant lots"—only separated the town from the pine forest—that great broad forest which extends uninterruptedly, and merely dotted with a few small corn and cotton fields, from Delaware to Louisiana.

Having some doubt about the road, I asked a direction of a man on horseback, who overtook and was passing me. In reply, he said it was a straight road, and we should go in company for a mile or two. He inquired if I was a stranger; and, when he heard that I was from the North, and now first visiting the South, he remarked that there was "no better place for me to go to than that for which I had inquired. Mr. X. was a very fine man—rich, got a splendid plantation, lived well, had plenty of company always, and there were a number of other show plantations near his. He reckoned I would visit some of them."

I asked what he meant by "show plantations." "Plantations belonging to rich people," he said, "where they had everything fixed up nice. There were several places that had that name; their owners always went out and lived on them part of the year, and kept a kind of open house, and were always ready to receive company. He reckoned I might go and stay a month round on them kind of places on——River, and it would not cost me a cent. They always had a great many Northerners going to see them, those gentlemen had. Almost every Northerner that came here was invited right out to visit some of them; and, in summer, a good many of them went to the North themselves."

(It was not till long afterwards, long after the above paragraph was first printed, that I fully comprehended the significance of the statement, that on the show plantations it would not cost me a cent.)[2]

During the forenoon my road continued broad and straight, and I was told that it was the chief outlet and thoroughfare of a very extensive agricultural district. There was very little land in cultivation within sight of the road, however; not a mile of it fenced, in twenty, and the only houses were log-cabins. The soil varied from a coarse, clean, yellow sand, to a dark, brown, sandy loam. There were indications that much of the land had, at some time, been under cultivation — had been worn out, and deserted.

Long teams of mules, driven by negroes, toiled slowly towards the town, with loads of rice or cotton. A stage-coach, with six horses to drag it through the heavy road, covered me, as it passed, with dust; and once or twice, I met a stylish carriage with fashionably-clad gentlemen and ladies, and primly-liveried negro-servants; but much the greatest traffic of the road was done by small one-horse carts, driven by white men, or women.

[2] Olmsted did not realize until later that northern visitors were welcomed only on certain "show plantations," designed to impress outside observers. The implication is that such selective site visits perhaps shielded him and others from seeing less well-ordered operations or less optimal conditions for slaves.

16. VISIT TO A RICE PLANTATION

After riding a few miles further I reached my destination.

Mr. X. has two plantations on the river, besides a large tract of poor pine forest land, extending some miles back upon the upland, and reaching above the malarious region. In the upper part of this pine land is a house, occupied by his overseer during the malarious season, when it is dangerous for any but negroes to remain during the night in the vicinity of the swamps or rice-fields. Even those few who have been born in the region, and have grown up subject to the malaria, are said to be generally weakly and short-lived. The negroes do not enjoy as good health on rice plantations as elsewhere; and the greater difficulty with which their lives are preserved, through infancy especially, shows that the subtle poison of the miasma is not innocuous to them; but Mr. X. boasts a steady increase of his negro stock, of five per cent. per annum, which is better than is averaged on the plantations of the interior.

The plantation which contains Mr. X.'s winter residence has but a small extent of rice-land, the greater part of it being reclaimed upland swamp soil, suitable for the culture of Sea Island cotton. The other plantation contains over five hundred acres of rice-land, fitted for irrigation; the remainder is unusually fertile reclaimed upland swamp, and some hundred acres of it are cultivated for maize and Sea Island cotton.

There is a "negro settlement" on each; but both plantations, although a mile or two apart, are worked together as one, under one overseer — the hands being drafted from one to another as their labour is required. Somewhat over seven hundred acres are at the present time under the plough in the two plantations: the whole number of negroes is two hundred, and they are reckoned to be equal to about one hundred prime hands — an unusual strength for that number of all classes. The overseer lives, in winter, near the settlement of the larger plantation, Mr. X. near that of the smaller.

It is an old family estate, inherited by Mr. X.'s wife, who, with her children, was born and brought up upon it in close intimacy with the negroes, a large proportion of whom were also included in her inheritance, or have been since born upon the estate. Mr. X. himself is a New England farmer's son, and has been a successful merchant and manufacturer [in Rhode Island].

The patriarchal institution should be seen here under its most favourable aspects; not only from the ties of long family association, common traditions, common memories, and, if ever, common interests, between the slaves and their rulers, but, also, from the practical talent for organization and administration, gained among the rugged fields, the complicated looms, and the exact and comprehensive counting-houses of New England, which directs the labour.

The house-servants are more intelligent, understand and perform their duties better, and are more appropriately dressed, than any I have seen before. The labour required of them is light, and they are treated with much more consideration for their health and comfort than is usually given to that of free domestics. They live in brick cabins, adjoining the house and stables, and one of these, into which I have looked, is neatly and comfortably furnished. Several of the house-servants, as is usual, are mulattoes, and good-looking. The mulattoes are generally preferred for in-door occupations. Slaves brought up to house-work dread to be employed at field-labour; and those accustomed to the comparatively unconstrained life of the negro-settlement, detest the close control and careful movements required of the house-servants. It is a punishment for a lazy field-hand, to employ him in menial duties at the house, as it is to set a sneaking sailor to do the work of a cabin-servant; and it is equally a punishment to a neglectful house-servant, to banish him to the field-gangs. All the household economy is, of course, carried on in a style appropriate to a wealthy gentleman's residence — not more so, nor less so, that I observe, than in an establishment of similar grade at the North.

It is a custom with Mr. X., when on the estate, to look each day at all the work going on, inspect the buildings, boats, embankments, and sluice-ways, and examine the sick. Yesterday I accompanied him in one of these daily rounds.

After a ride of several miles through the woods, in the rear of the plantations we came to his largest negro-settlement. There was a street, or common, two hundred feet wide, on which the cabins of the negroes fronted. Each cabin was a framed building, the walls boarded and white-washed on the outside, lathed and plastered within, the roof shingled; forty-two feet long, twenty-one feet wide, divided into two family ten-ements, each twenty-one by twenty-one; each tenement divided into three rooms—one, the common household apartment, twenty-one by ten; each of the others (bedrooms), ten by ten. There was a brick fire-place in the middle of the long side of each living room, the chimneys rising in one, in the middle of the roof. Besides these rooms, each tene-ment had a cock-loft [small attic], entered by steps from the household room. Each tenement is occupied, on an average, by five persons. There were in them closets, with locks and keys, and a varying quantity of rude furniture. Each cabin stood two hundred feet from the next, and the street in front of them being two hundred feet wide, they were just that distance apart each way. The people were nearly all absent at work, and had locked their outer doors, taking the keys with them. Each cabin has a front and back door, and each room a window, closed by a wooden shutter, swinging outward, on hinges. Between each tenement and the next house, is a small piece of ground, inclosed with palings, in which are coops of fowl with chickens, hovels for nests, and for sows with pig. There were a great many fowls in the street. The negroes' swine are allowed to run in the woods, each owner having his own distinguished by a peculiar mark. In the rear of the yards were gardens—a half-acre to each family. Internally the cabins appeared dirty and disordered, which was rather a pleasant indication that their home-life was not much inter-fered with, though I found certain police regulations were enforced.

The cabin nearest the overseer's house was used as a nursery. Having driven up to this, Mr. X. inquired first of an old nurse how the children were; whether there had been any births since his last visit; spoke to two convalescent young mothers, who were lounging on the floor of the portico, with the children. . . .

. . . On the verandah and the steps of the nursery, there were twenty-seven children, most of them infants, that had been left there by their mothers, while they were working their tasks in the fields. They probably make a visit to them once or twice during the day, to nurse them, and receive them to take to their cabins, or where they like, when they have finished their tasks—generally in the middle of the afternoon. The older children were fed with porridge, by the general nurse. A number of girls, eight or ten years old, were occupied in holding and tending the youngest infants. Those a little older—the crawlers—were in the pen, and those big enough to toddle were playing on the steps, or before the house. Some of these, with two or three bigger ones, were singing and dancing about a fire that they had made on the ground. They were not at all disturbed or interrupted in their amusement by the presence of their owner and myself. At twelve years of age, the children are first put to regular field-work; until then no labour is required of them, except, perhaps, occasionally they are charged with some light kind of duty, such as frightening birds from corn. When first sent to the field, one quarter of an able-bodied hand's day's work is ordinarily allotted to them, as their task.

From the settlement, we drove to the "mill"—not a flouring mill, though I believe there is a run of stones in it—but a monster barn, with more extensive and better machinery for threshing and storing rice, driven by a steam-engine, than I have ever seen used for grain before. Adjoining the mill-house were shops and sheds, in which blacksmiths, carpenters, and other mechanics—all slaves, belonging to Mr. X.—were at work. He called my attention to the excellence of their workmanship, and said that they exercised as much ingenuity and skill as the ordinary mechanics that he was used to employ in New England. He pointed out to me some carpenter's work, a part of which had been executed by a New England mechanic, and a part by one of his own hands, which indicated that the latter was much the better workman.

I was gratified by this, for I had been so often told, in Virginia, by gentlemen anxious to convince me that the negro was incapable of being educated or improved to a condition in which it would be safe to trust him with himself—that no negro-mechanic could ever be taught, or induced to work carefully or nicely—that I had begun to believe it might be so.

17. THE "WATCHMAN"

We were attended through the mill-house by a respectable-looking, orderly, and quiet-mannered mulatto, who was called, by his master, "the watchman." His duties, however, as they were described to me, were those of a steward, or intendant. He carried, by a strap at his waist, a very large number of keys, and had charge of all stores of provisions, tools, and materials of the plantations, as well as of all their produce, before it was shipped to market. He weighed and measured out all the rations of the slaves and the cattle; superintended the mechanics, and made and repaired, as was necessary, all the machinery, including the steam-engine.

In all these departments, his authority was superior to that of the overseer. The overseer received his private allowance of family provisions from him, as did also the head-servant at the mansion, who was his brother. His responsibility was much greater than that of the overseer; and Mr. X. said he would trust him with much more than he would any overseer he had ever known.

Anxious to learn how this trustworthiness and intelligence, so unusual in a slave, had been developed or ascertained, I inquired of his history, which was briefly as follows.

Being the son of a favourite house-servant, he had been, as a child, associated with the white family, and received by chance something of the early education of the white children. When old enough, he had been employed, for some years, as a waiter; but, at his own request, was eventually allowed to learn the blacksmith's trade, in the plantation shop. Showing ingenuity and talent, he was afterwards employed to make and repair the plantation cotton-gins. Finally, his owner took him to a steam-engine builder, and paid $500 to have him instructed as a machinist. After he had become a skilful workman, he obtained employment as an engineer; and for some years continued in this occupation, and was allowed to spend his wages for himself. Finding, however, that he was acquiring dissipated habits, and wasting his earnings, Mr. X. eventually brought him, much against his inclinations, back to the plantations. Being allowed peculiar privileges, and given duties wholly flattering to his self-respect, he soon became contented; and, of course was able to be extremely valuable to his owner. . . .

The watchman was a fine-looking fellow: as we were returning from church, on Sunday, he had passed us, well dressed and well mounted, and as he raised his hat, to salute us, there was nothing in his manner or appearance, except his colour, to distinguish him from a gentleman of good breeding and fortune.

When we were leaving the house, to go to church, on Sunday, after all the white family had entered their carriages, or mounted their horses, the head house-servant also mounted a horse — as he did so, slipping a coin into the hands of the boy who had been holding him. Afterwards, we passed a family of negroes, in a light waggon, the oldest among them driving the horse. On my inquiring if the slaves were allowed to take horses to drive to church, I was informed that in each of these three cases, the horses belonged to the negroes who were driving or riding them. The old man was infirm, and Mr. X. had given him a horse, to enable him to move about. He was probably employed to look after the cattle at pasture, or at something in which it was necessary, for his use-fulness, that he should have a horse: I say this, because I afterwards found, in similar cases on other plantations, that it was so. But the watch-man and the house-servant had bought their horses with money. The watchman was believed to own three horses; and, to account for his wealth, Mr. X.'s son told me that his father considered him a very valu-able servant, and frequently encouraged his good behaviour with hand-some gratuities. He receives, probably, considerably higher wages, in fact (in the form of presents), than the white overseer. He knew his father gave him two hundred dollars at once, a short time ago. The watchman has a private house, and, no doubt, lives in considerable luxury.

Will it be said, "therefore, Slavery is neither necessarily degrading nor inhumane"? On the other hand, so far as it is not, there is no apol-ogy for it. It is possible, though not probable, that this fine fellow, if he had been born a free man, would be no better employed than he is here; but, in that case, where is the advantage? Certainly not in the economy of the arrangement. And if he were self-dependent, if, especially, he had to provide for the present and future of those he loved, and was able to do so, would he not necessarily live a happier, stronger, better, and more respectable man?

18. THE TASK SYSTEM AND RICE CULTIVATION

After passing through tool-rooms, corn-rooms, mule-stables, store-rooms, and a large garden, in which vegetables to be distributed among the negroes, as well as for the family, are grown, we walked to the rice-land. It is divided by embankments into fields of about twenty acres each, but varying somewhat in size, according to the course of the river. The arrangements are such that each field may be flooded independ-ently of the rest, and they are subdivided by open ditches into rectangular plats [plots] of a quarter acre each. We first proceeded to where twenty or thirty women and girls were engaged in raking together, in heaps and winrows [windrows], the stubble and rubbish left on the field after the last crop, and burning it. The main object of this operation is to kill all the seeds of weeds, or of rice, on the ground. Ordinarily it is done by tasks—a certain number of the small divisions of the field being given to each hand to burn in a day; but owing to a more than usual amount of rain having fallen lately, and some other causes, making the work harder in some places than others, the women were now working by the [hour], under the direction of a "driver," a negro man, who walked about among them, taking care that they left nothing unburned. . . .

In the next field, twenty men, or boys, for none of them looked as if they were full-grown, were ploughing, each with a single mule, and a light, New-York-made plough. The soil was friable [easily crumbled], the ploughing easy, and the mules proceeded at a smart pace; the furrows were straight, regular, and well turned. Their task was nominally an acre and a quarter a day; somewhat less actually, as the measure includes the space occupied by the ditches, which are two to three feet wide, running around each quarter of an acre. The ploughing gang was superintended by a driver, who was provided with a watch; and while we were looking at them he called out that it was twelve o'clock. The mules were immediately taken from the ploughs, and the plough-boys mounting them, leapt the ditches, and cantered off to the stables, to feed them. One or two were ordered to take their ploughs to the blacksmith, for repairs. . . .

Leaving the rice-land, we went next to some of the upland fields, where we found several other gangs of negroes at work; one entirely of men engaged in ditching; another of women, and another of boys and girls, "listing" [cultivating] an old corn-field with hoes. All of them were working by tasks, and were overlooked by negro drivers. They all laboured with greater rapidity and cheerfulness than any slaves I have before seen; and the women struck their hoes as if they were strong, and well able to engage in muscular labour. The expression of their faces was generally repulsive, and their *ensemble* [clothing] anything but agreeable. The dress of most was uncouth and cumbrous, dirty and ragged; reefed up, as I have once before described, at the hips, so as to show their heavy legs, wrapped round with a piece of old blanket, in lieu of leggings or stockings. Most of them worked with bare arms, but wore strong shoes on their feet, and handkerchiefs on their heads; some of them were smoking, and each gang had a fire burning on the ground, near where they were at work, by which to light their

pipes and warm their breakfast. Mr. X. said this was always their custom, even in summer. To each gang a boy or girl was also attached,
whose business it was to bring water for them to drink, and to go for
anything required by the driver. . . .

The field-hands are all divided into four classes, according to their
physical capacities. The children beginning as "quarter-hands," advanc-
ing to "half-hands," and then to "three-quarter hands"; and, finally, when
mature, and able-bodied, healthy, and strong, to "full hands." As they
decline in strength, from age, sickness, or other cause, they retrograde
in the scale, and proportionately less labour is required of them. Many,
of naturally weak frame, never are put among the full hands. Finally,
the aged are left out at the annual classification, and no more regular
field-work is required of them, although they are generally provided
with some light, sedentary occupation. I saw one old woman picking
"tailings" of rice out of a heap of chaff, an occupation at which she was
probably not earning her salt. Mr. X. told me she was a native African,
having been brought when a girl from the Guinea coast. She spoke
almost unintelligibly; but after some other conversation, in which I had
not been able to understand a word she said, he jokingly proposed to
send her back to Africa. She expressed her preference to remain where
she was, very emphatically. "Why?" She did not answer readily, but
being pressed, threw up her palsied hands, and said furiously, "I lubs
'ou, mas'r, oh, I lubs 'ou. I don't want go 'way from 'ou."

The field-hands are nearly always worked in gangs, the strength of a
gang varying according to the work that engages it; usually it numbers
twenty or more, and is directed by a driver. As on most large plantations, whether of rice or cotton, in Eastern Georgia and South Carolina,
nearly all ordinary and regular work is performed *by tasks*: that is to
say, each hand has his labour for the day marked out before him, and
can take his own time to do it in. For instance, in making drains in light,
clean meadow land, each man or woman of the full hands is required to
dig one thousand cubic feet; in swamp-land that is being prepared for
rice culture, where there are not many stumps, the task for a ditcher is
five hundred feet: while in a very strong cypress swamp, only two hundred feet is required; in hoeing rice, a certain number of rows, equal to
one-half or two-thirds of an acre, according to the condition of the land;
in sowing rice (strewing in drills), two acres; in reaping rice (if it stands
well), three-quarters of an acre; or, sometimes a gang will be required to
reap, tie in sheaves, and carry to the stack-yard the produce of a certain
area, commonly equal to one fourth the number of acres that there are
hands working together. . . .

These are the tasks for first-class able-bodied men; they are lessened by one quarter for three-quarter hands, and proportionately for the lighter classes. In allotting the tasks, the drivers are expected to put the weaker hands where (if there is any choice in the appearance of the ground, as where certain rows in hoeing corn would be less weedy than others,) they will be favoured.

These tasks certainly would not be considered excessively hard, by a Northern labourer; and, in point of fact, the more industrious and active hands finish them often by two o'clock. I saw one or two leaving the field soon after one o'clock, several about two; and between three and four, I met a dozen women and several men coming home to their cabins, having finished their day's work. . . .

It is the driver's duty to make the tasked hands do their work well. If, in their haste to finish it, they neglect to do it properly, he "sets them back," so that carelessness will hinder more than it will hasten the completion of their tasks.

19. PORTRAIT OF AN OVERSEER

Mr. X. considers his overseer an uncommonly efficient and faithful one, but he would not employ him, even during the summer, when he is absent for several months, if the law did not require it.[1] He has sometimes left his plantation in care of one of the drivers for a considerable length of time, after having discharged an overseer; and he thinks it has then been quite as well conducted as ever. His overseer consults the drivers on all important points, and is governed by their advice.

Mr. X. said, that though overseers sometimes punished the negroes severely, and otherwise ill-treated them, it is their more common fault to indulge them foolishly in their disposition to idleness, or in other ways to curry favour with them, so they may not inform the proprietor of their own misconduct or neglect. He has his overseer bound to certain rules, by written contract; and it is stipulated that he can discharge him at any moment, without remuneration for his loss of time and inconvenience, if he should at any time be dissatisfied with him. One of the rules is, that he shall never punish a negro with his own hands, and that corporeal punishment, when necessary, shall be inflicted by the drivers. The advantage of this is, that it secures time for deliberation, and prevents

---

[1] The slave codes for several states, including those for Virginia (which Olmsted seems to have been most familiar with) and Georgia, mandated the presence of an owner or overseer on plantations with slaveholdings over a certain number of slaves.

punishment being made in sudden passion. His drivers are not allowed to carry their whips with them in the field; so that if the overseer wishes a hand punished, it is necessary to call a driver; and the driver has then to go to his cabin, which is, perhaps, a mile or two distant, to get his whip, before it can be applied.

I asked how often the necessity of punishment occurred.

"Sometimes, perhaps, not once for two or three weeks; then it will seem as if the devil had got into them all, and there is a good deal of it."

20. SLAVES AS SELLERS AND THIEVES

As the negroes finish the labour required of them by Mr. X., at three or four o'clock in the afternoon, they can employ the remainder of the day in labouring for themselves, if they choose. Each family has a half-acre of land allotted to it, for a garden; besides which, there is a large vegetable garden, cultivated by a gardener for the plantation, from which they are supplied, to a greater or less extent. They are at liberty to sell whatever they choose from the products of their own garden, and to make what they can by keeping swine and fowls. Mr. X.'s family have no other supply of poultry and eggs than what is obtained by purchase from his own negroes; they frequently, also, purchase game from them. The only restriction upon their traffic is a "liquor law." They are not allowed to buy or sell ardent spirits. This prohibition, like liquor laws elsewhere, unfortunately, cannot be enforced; and, of late years, grog-shops, at which stolen goods are bought from the slaves, and poisonous liquors—chiefly the worst whisky, much watered and made stupefying by an infusion of tobacco—are clandestinely sold to them, have become an established evil, and the planters find themselves almost powerless to cope with it. They have, here, lately organized an association for this purpose, and have brought several offenders to trial; but, as it is a penitentiary offence, the culprit spares no pains or expense to avoid conviction—and it is almost impossible, in a community of which so large a proportion is poor and degraded, to have a jury sufficiently honest and intelligent to permit the law to be executed.

A remarkable illustration of this evil has lately occurred. A planter, discovering that a considerable quantity of cotton had been stolen from him, informed the patrol of the neighbouring planters of it. A stratagem was made use of, to detect the thief, and, what was of much more importance—there being no question but that this was a slave—to discover for whom the thief worked. A lot of cotton was prepared, by mixing hair with it, and put in a tempting place. A negro was seen to take it, and was followed by scouts to a grog-shop, several miles distant, where he sold it—its real value being nearly ten dollars—for ten cents, taking his pay in liquor. The [shopkeeper] was arrested, and, the theft being made to appear, by the hair, before a justice, obtained bail in $2,000, to answer at the higher court. Some of the best legal counsel of the State has been engaged, to obtain, if possible, his conviction.

This difficulty in the management of slaves is a great and very rapidly increasing one. Everywhere that I have been, I have found the planters provoked and angry about it. A swarm of Jews, within the last ten years, has settled in nearly every Southern town, many of them men of no character, opening cheap clothing and trinket shops; ruining, or driving out of business, many of the old retailers, and engaging in an unlawful trade with the simple negroes, which is found very profitable.

The law which prevents the reception of the evidence of a negro in courts, here strikes back, with a most annoying force, upon the dominant power itself. In the mischief thus arising, we see a striking illustration of the danger which stands before the South, whenever its prosperity shall invite extensive immigration, and lead what would otherwise be a healthy competition to flow through its channels of industry. . . .

Mr. X. remarks that his arrangements allow his servants no excuse for dealing with these fellows. He has a rule to purchase everything they desire to sell, and to give them a high price for it himself. Eggs constitute a circulating medium on the plantation. Their par value is considered to be twelve for a dime, at which they may always be exchanged for cash, or left on deposit, without interest, at his kitchen.

21. MOVING TOWARD FREEDOM

The ascertained practicability of thus dealing with slaves, together with the obvious advantages of the method of working them by tasks, which I have described, seem to me to indicate that it is not so impracticable as is generally supposed, if only it was desired by those having the power, to rapidly extinguish Slavery, and while doing so, to educate the negro for taking care of himself, in freedom. Let, for instance, any slave be provided with all things he will demand, as far as practicable, and charge him for them at certain prices—honest, market prices for his necessities, higher prices for harmless luxuries, and excessive, but not absolutely prohibitory, prices for everything likely to do him harm. Credit him, at a fixed price, for every day's work he does, and for all above a certain easily accomplished task in a day, at an increased price, so that his reward will be in an increasing ratio to his perseverance. Let the prices of provisions be so proportioned to the price of task-work, that it will be about as easy as it is now for him to obtain a bare subsistence. When he has no food and shelter due to him, let him be confined in solitude, or otherwise punished, until he asks for opportunity to earn exemption from punishment by labour.

When he desires to marry, and can persuade any woman to marry him, let the two be dealt with as in partnership. Thus, a young man or young woman will be attractive somewhat in proportion to his or her reputation for industry and providence [thrift]. Thus industry and providence will become fashionable. Oblige them to purchase food for their children, and let them have the benefit of their children's labour, and they will be careful to teach their children to avoid waste, and to honour labour. Let those who have not gained credit while hale and young, sufficient to support themselves in comfort when prevented by age or infirmity from further labour, be supported by a tax upon all the negroes of the plantation, or of a community. Improvidence, and pretence of inability to labour, will then be disgraceful.

When any man has a balance to his credit equal to his value as a slave, let that constitute him a free man. It will be optional with him and his employer whether he shall continue longer in the relation of servant. If desirable for both that he should, it is probable that he will; for unless he is honest, prudent, industrious, and discreet, he will not have acquired the means of purchasing his freedom.

If he is so, he will remain where he is, unless he is more wanted elsewhere; a fact that will be established by his being called away by higher wages, or the prospect of greater ease and comfort elsewhere. If he is so drawn off, it is better for all parties concerned that he should go. Better for his old master; for he would not refuse him sufficient wages to induce him to stay, unless he could get the work he wanted him to do done cheaper than he would justly do it. Poor wages would certainly, in the long ran, buy but poor work; fair wages, fair work. . . .

Married persons, of course, can only become free together. In the appraisement of their value, let that of their young children be included, so that they cannot be parted from them; but with regard to children old enough to earn something more than their living, let it be optional what they do for them.

Such a system would simply combine the commendable elements of the emancipation law of Cuba,[1] and those of the reformatory punishment system, now in successful operation in some of the British penal colonies, with a few practical modifications. Further modifications would, doubtless, be needed, which any man who has had much practical experience in dealing with slaves might readily suggest. . . .

Education in theology and letters could be easily combined with such a plan as I have hinted at; or, if a State should wish to encourage the improvement of its negro constituent—as, in the progress of enlightenment and Christianity, may be hoped to eventually occur—a simple provision of the law, making a certain standard of proficiency the condition of political freedom, would probably create a natural demand for education, which commerce, under its inexorable higher laws, would be obliged to satisfy.

I do not think, after all I have heard to favour it, that there is any good reason to consider the negro, naturally and essentially, the moral inferior of the white; or, that if he is so, it is in those elements of character which should for ever prevent us from trusting him with equal social munities [privileges] with ourselves.

[1] [Olmsted] In Cuba every slave has the privilege of emancipating himself, by paying a price which does not depend upon the selfish exactions of the masters; but it is either a fixed price, or else is fixed, in each case, by disinterested appraisers. The consequence is, that emancipations are constantly going on, and the free people of colour are becoming enlightened, cultivated, and wealthy. In no part of the United States do they occupy the high social position which they enjoy in Cuba.

22. PLANTATION RELIGION

On most of the large rice plantations which I have seen in this vicinity, there is a small chapel, which the negroes call their prayer-house. The owner of one of these told me that, having furnished the prayer-house with seats having a back-rail, his negroes petitioned him to remove it, because it did not leave them *room enough to pray*. It was explained to me that it is their custom, in social worship, to work themselves up to a great pitch of excitement, in which they yell and cry aloud, and finally, shriek and leap up, clapping their hands and dancing, as it is done at heathen festivals. The back-rail they found to seriously impede this exercise.

Mr. X. told me that he had endeavoured, with but little success, to prevent this shouting and jumping of the negroes at their meetings on his plantation, from a conviction that there was not the slightest element of religious sentiment in it. He considered it to be engaged in more as an exciting amusement than from any really religious impulse. In the town churches, except, perhaps, those managed and conducted almost exclusively by negroes, the slaves are said to commonly engage in religious exercises in a sober and decorous manner; yet, a member of a Presbyterian church in a Southern city told me, that he had seen the negroes in his own house of worship, during "a season of revival," leap from their seats, throw their arms wildly in the air, shout vehemently and unintelligibly, cry, groan, rend their clothes, and fall into cataleptic trances.

On almost every large plantation, and in every neighbourhood of small ones, there is one man who has come to be considered the head or pastor of the local church. The office among the negroes, as among all other people, confers a certain importance and power. A part of the reverence attaching to the duties is given to the person; vanity and self-confidence are cultivated, and a higher ambition aroused than can usually enter the mind of a slave. The self-respect of the preacher is also often increased by the consideration in which he is held by his master, as well as by his fellows; thus, the preachers generally have an air of superiority to other negroes; they acquire a remarkable memory of words, phrases, and forms; a curious sort of poetic talent is developed, and a habit is obtained of rhapsodizing and exciting furious emotions, to a great degree spurious and temporary, in themselves and others, through the imagination. I was introduced, the other day, to a preacher, who was represented to be quite distinguished among them. I took his hand, respectfully, and said I was happy to meet him. He seemed to take this for a joke, and laughed heartily. He was a "driver," and my friend said—

"He drives the negroes at the cotton all the week, and Sundays he drives them at the Gospel—don't you, Ned?" . . .

A majority of the public houses of worship at the South are small, rude structures of logs, or rough boards, built by the united labour or contributions of the people of a large neighbourhood or district of country, and are used as places of assembly for all public purposes. Few of them have any regular clergymen, but preachers of different denominations go from one to another, sometimes in a defined rotation, or "circuit," so that they may be expected at each of their stations at regular intervals. A late report of the Southern Aid Society states that hardly one-fifth of the preachers are regularly educated for their business, and that "you would starve a host of them if you debarred them from seeking additional support for their families by worldly occupation." In one presbytery of the Presbyterian Church, which is, perhaps, the richest, and includes the most educated body of people of all the Southern Churches, there are twenty-one ministers whose wages are not over two hundred and fifty dollars each. The proportion of ministers, of all sorts, to people, is estimated at one to thirteen hundred. (In the Free States it is estimated at one to nine hundred.) The report of this Society also states, that "within the limits of the United States religious destitution lies comparatively at the South and South-west, and that from the first settlement of the country the North has preserved a decided religious superiority over the South, especially in three important particulars: in ample supply of Christian institutions; extensive supply of Christian truth; and thorough Christian regimen, both in the Church and in the community." It is added that, "while the South-western States have always needed a stronger arm of the Christian ministry to raise them up toward a Christian equality with their Northern brethren, their supply in this respect has always been decidedly inferior." The reason of this is the same with that which explains the general ignorance of the people of the South: The effect of Slavery in preventing social association of the whites, and in encouraging vagabond and improvident habits of life among the poor.

The two largest denominations of Christians at the South are the Methodists and Baptists—the last having a numerical superiority. There are some subdivisions of each, and of the Baptists especially, the nature of which I do not understand. Two grand divisions of the Baptists are known as the Hard Shells and the Soft Shells. There is an intense rivalry and jealousy among these various sects and sub-sects, and the controversy between them is carried on with a bitterness and persistence exceeding anything which I have known at the North, and in a manner which curiously indicates how the terms Christianity, piety, etc., are misapplied to partisanship and conditions of the imagination.

23. A BI-RACIAL SUNDAY SERVICE

The religious service which I am about to describe, was held in a less than usually rude meeting-house, the boards by which it was enclosed being planed, the windows glazed, and the seats for the white people provided with backs. It stood in a small clearing of the woods, and there was no habitation within two miles of it. When I reached it with my friends, the services had already commenced. Fastened to trees, in a circle about the house, there were many saddled horses and mules, and a few attached to carts or waggons. There were two smouldering camp-fires, around which sat circles of negroes and white boys, roasting potatoes in the ashes.

In the house were some fifty white people, generally dressed in homespun, and of the class called "crackers," though I was told that some of them owned a good many negroes, and were by no means so poor as their appearance indicated. About one-third of the house, at the end opposite the desk, was covered by a gallery or cock-loft, under and in which, distinctly separated from the whites, was a dense body of negroes; the men on one side, the women on another. The whites were seated promiscuously in the body of the house.

The negroes present outnumbered the whites, but the exercises at this time seemed to have no reference to them; there were many more waiting about the doors outside, and they were expecting to enjoy a meeting to themselves, after the whites had left the house. They were generally neatly dressed, more so than the majority of the whites present, but in a distinctly plantation or slave style. A few of them wore somewhat expensive articles, evidently of their own selection and purchase; but I observed with some surprise, that not one of the women had a bonnet upon her head, all wearing handkerchiefs, generally of gay patterns, and becomingly arranged. . . .

The preliminary devotional exercises—a Scripture reading, singing, and painfully irreverential and meaningless harangues nominally addressed to the Deity, but really to the audience—being concluded, the sermon was commenced by reading a text, with which, however, it had, so far as I could discover, no further association. Without often being violent in his manner, the speaker nearly all the time cried aloud at the utmost stretch of his voice, as if calling to some one a long distance off; as his discourse was extemporaneous, however, he sometimes returned with curious effect to his natural conversational tone; and as he was gifted with a strong imagination, and possessed of a good deal of dramatic power, he kept the attention of the people very well. There was no argument upon any point that the congregation were likely to have much difference of opinion upon, nor any special connection between one sentence and another. . . . The audience were frequently reminded that the preacher did not want their attention for any purpose of his own; but that he demanded a respectful hearing as "the ambassador of Christ." He had the habit of frequently repeating a phrase, or of bringing forward the same idea in a slightly different form, a great many times. The following passage, of which I took notes, presents an example of this, followed by one of the best instances of his dramatic talent that occurred. He was leaning far over the desk, with his arm stretched forward, gesticulating violently, yelling at the highest key, and catching breath with an effort:—

"A—ah! why don't you come to Christ? ah! what's the reason? ah! Is it because he was of *lowly birth?* ah! Is that it? *Is it* because he was born in a manger? ah! Is it because he was of a humble origin? ah! Is it because he was lowly born? a-ha! Is it because, ah!—is it because, ah!—because he was called a Nazarene? Is it because he was born in a stable?—or is it because—because he was of humble origin? Or is it—is it because"—He drew back, and after a moment's silence put his hand to his chin, and began walking up and down the platform of the pulpit, soliloquizing. "It can't be—it can't be—?" Then lifting his eyes and gradually turning towards the audience, while he continued to speak in a low, thoughtful tone: "Perhaps you don't like the messenger—is that the reason? I'm the ambassador of the great and glorious King; it's his invitation, 'taint mine. You mustn't mind me. I ain't no account. Suppose a ragged, insignificant little boy should come running in here and tell you, 'Mister, your house's a-fire!' would you mind the ragged, insignificant little boy, and refuse to listen to him, because he didn't look respectable?"

At the end of the sermon he stepped down from the pulpit, and, crossing the house towards the negroes, said, quietly, as he walked, "I take great interest in the poor blacks; and this evening I am going to hold a meeting specially for you." With this he turned back, and without reentering the pulpit, but strolling up and down before it, read a hymn, at the conclusion of which, he laid his book down, and speaking for a moment with natural emphasis, said—

"I don't want to create a tumultuous scene, now;—that isn't my intention. I don't want to make an excitement,—that aint what I want,—but I feel that there's some here that I may never see again, ah! and, as I may never have another opportunity, I feel it my duty as an ambassador of Jesus Christ, ah! before I go—" By this time he had returned to the high key and whining yell. Exactly what he felt it his duty to do, I did not understand; but evidently to employ some more powerful agency of awakening than arguments and appeals to the understanding; and, before I could conjecture, in the least, of what sort this was to be, while he was yet speaking calmly, deprecating excitement, my attention was attracted to several men, who had previously appeared sleepy and indifferent, but who now suddenly began to sigh, raise their heads, and *shed tears*—some standing up, so that they might be observed in doing this by the whole congregation—the tears running down their noses without any interruption. . . .

It was immediately evident that a large part of the audience understood his wish to be the reverse of what he had declared, and considered themselves called upon to assist him; and it was astonishing to see with what readiness the faces of those who, up to the moment he gave the signal, had appeared drowsy and stupid, were made to express distressing excitement, sighing, groaning, and weeping. Rising in their seats, and walking up to the pulpit, they grasped each other's hands agonizingly, and remained, some kneeling, others standing, with their faces towards the remainder of the assembly. There was great confusion and tumult, and the poor children, evidently impressed by the terrified tone of the howling preacher, with the expectation of some immediately impending calamity, shrieked, and ran hither and thither, till negro girls came forward, laughing at the imposition, and carried them out.

At length, when some twenty had gathered around the preacher, and it became evident that no more could be drawn out, he stopped a moment for breath, and then repeated a verse of a hymn, which being sung, he again commenced to cry aloud, calling now upon all the unconverted, who were *willing* to be saved, to kneel. A few did so, and another verse was sung, followed by another more fervent exhortation. So it went on; at each verse his entreaties, warnings, and threats, and the responsive groans, sobs, and ejaculations of his coterie grew louder and stronger. Those who refused to kneel were addressed as standing on the brink of the infernal pit, into which a diabolical divinity was momentarily on the point of satisfying the necessities of his character by hurling them off. . . .

The last verse of the hymn was sung. A comparatively quiet and sober repetition of Scripture phrases, strung together heterogeneously and without meaning, in the form of prayer, followed, a benediction was pronounced, and in five minutes all the people were out of the door, with no trace of the previous excitement left, but most of the men talking eagerly of the price of cotton, and negroes, and other news.

The negroes kept their place during all of the tumult; there may have been a sympathetic groan or exclamation uttered by one or two of them, but generally they expressed only the interest of curiosity in the proceedings, such as Europeans might at a performance of the dancing dervishes, an Indian pow-wow, or an exhibition of "psychological" or "spiritual" phenomena, making it very evident that the emotion of the performers was optionally engaged in, as an appropriate part of divine service. There was generally a self-satisfied smile upon their faces; and

I have no doubt they felt that they could do it with a good deal more energy and abandon, if they were called upon. I did not wish to detain my companion to witness how they succeeded, when their turn came; and I can only judge from the fact, that those I saw the next morning were so hoarse that they could scarcely speak, that the religious exercises they most enjoy are rather hard upon the lungs, whatever their effect may be upon the soul.

24. FROM SAVANNAH TO COLUMBUS

I left Savannah for the West, by the Macon road; the train started punctually to a second, at its advertised time; the speed was not great, but regular, and less time was lost unnecessarily, at way-stations, than usually on our Northern roads.

I have travelled more than five hundred miles on the Georgia roads, and I am glad to say that all of them seem to be exceedingly well managed. The speed upon them is not generally more than from fifteen to twenty miles an hour; but it is made, as advertised, with considerable punctuality. The roads are admirably engineered and constructed, and their equipment will compare favourably with that of any other roads on the continent. There are now upwards of twelve hundred miles of railroad in the State, and more building. The Savannah and Macon line—the first built—was commenced in 1834. . . . It has been always, in a great degree, under the management of Northern men—was engineered, and is still worked chiefly by Northern men, and a large amount of its stock is owned at the North. I am told that most of the mechanics, and of the successful merchants and tradesmen of Savannah came originally from the North, or are the sons of Northern men.

Partly by rail and partly by rapid stage-coaching (the coaches, horses, and drivers again from the North), I crossed the State in about twenty-four hours. The railroad is since entirely completed from Savannah to Montgomery, in Alabama, and is being extended slowly towards the Mississippi; of course with the expectation that it will eventually reach the Pacific, and thus make Savannah "the gate to the commerce of the world." Ship-masters will hope that, when either it or its rival in South Carolina has secured that honour, they will succeed, better than they yet have done, in removing the bars, physical and legal, by which commerce is now annoyed in its endeavours to serve them.

At Columbus, I spent several days. It is the largest manufacturing town, south of Richmond, in the Slave States. It is situated at the Falls, and the head of steamboat navigation of the Chattahoochee, the western boundary of Georgia. The water-power is sufficient to drive two hundred thousand spindles, with a proportionate number of looms. There are, probably, at present from fifteen to twenty thousand spindles running. The operatives in the cotton-mills are said to be mainly "Cracker girls" (poor whites from the country), who earn, in good times, by piecework, from $8 to $12 a month. There are, besides the cotton-mills, one woollen-mill, one paper-mill, a foundry, a cotton-gin factory, a machine-shop, etc. The labourers in all these are mainly whites, and they are in such a condition that, if temporarily thrown out of employment, great numbers of them are at once reduced to a state of destitution, and are dependent upon credit or charity for their daily food. Public entertainments were being held at the time of my visit, the profits to be applied to the relief of operatives in mills which had been stopped by the effects of a late flood of the river. Yet Slavery is constantly boasted to be a perfect safeguard against such distress.

I had seen in no place, since I left Washington, so much gambling, intoxication, and cruel treatment of servants in public, as in Columbus. This, possibly, was accidental; but I must caution persons, travelling for health or pleasure, to avoid stopping in the town. The hotel in which I lodged was disgustingly dirty; the table revolting; the waiters stupid, inattentive, and annoying. It was the stage-house; but I was informed that the other public-house was no better. There are very good inns at Macon, and at Montgomery, Alabama; and it will be best for an invalid proceeding from Savannah westward, if possible, not to spend a night between these towns.

25. STEAMBOAT FROM MONTGOMERY TO MOBILE

A day's journey took me from Columbus, through a hilly wilderness, with a few dreary villages, and many isolated cotton farms, with comfortless habitations for black and white upon them, to Montgomery, the capital of Alabama.

Montgomery is a prosperous town, with pleasant suburbs, and a remarkably enterprising population, among which there is a considerable proportion of Northern and foreign-born business-men and mechanics.

I spent a week here, and then left for Mobile, on the steamboat Fashion, a clean and well-ordered boat, with polite and obliging officers. We were two days and a half making the passage, the boat stopping at almost every bluff and landing to take on cotton, until she had a freight of nineteen hundred bales, which was built up on the guards, seven or eight tiers in height, and until it reached the hurricane deck. The boat was thus brought so deep that her guards were in the water, and the ripple of the river constantly washed over them. There are two hundred landings on the Alabama River, and three hundred on the Bigby (Tombeckbee [Tombigbee] of the geographers), at which the boats advertise to call, if required, for passengers or freight. This, of course, makes the passage exceedingly tedious. The so-called landings, however, have not in many cases the slightest artificial accommodations for the purpose of a landing. The boat's hawser [cable for mooring], if used, is made fast to a living tree; there is not a sign of a wharf, often no house in sight, and sometimes no distinct road.

The principal town at which we landed was Selma, a pleasant village, in one corner of which I came upon a tall, ill-proportioned, broken-windowed brick barrack; it had no grounds about it, was close upon the highway, was in every way dirty, neglected, and forlorn in expression. I inquired what it was, and was answered, the "Young Ladies' College." There were a number of pretty private gardens in the town, in which I noticed several evergreen oaks, the first I had seen since leaving Savannah. . . .

There were about one hundred passengers on the Fashion, besides a number of poor people and negroes on the lower deck. They were, generally, cotton-planters, going to Mobile on business, or emigrants bound to Texas or Arkansas. They were usually well dressed, but were a rough, coarse style of people, drinking a great deal, and most of the time under a little alcoholic excitement. Not sociable, except when the topics of cotton, land, and negroes, were started; interested, however, in talk about theatres and the turf; very profane; often showing the handles of concealed weapons about their persons, but not quarrelsome, avoiding disputes and altercations, and respectful to one another in forms of words; very ill-informed, except on plantation business; their language ungrammatical, idiomatic, and extravagant. Their grand characteristics—simplicity of motives, vague, shallow, and purely objective habits of thought; and bold, self-reliant movement.

With all their individual independence, I soon could perceive a very great homogeneousness of character, by which they were distinguishable from any other people with whom I had before been thrown in contact; and I began to study it with interest, as the Anglo-Saxon development of the South-west.

I found that, more than any people I had ever seen, they were unrateable by dress, taste, forms, and expenditures. I was perplexed by finding, apparently united in the same individual, the self-possession, confidence, and the use of expressions of deference, of the well-equipped gentleman, and the coarseness and low tastes of the uncivilized boor—frankness and reserve, recklessness and self-restraint, extravagance, and penuriousness.

26. CONVERSATION WITH A RED RIVER "COTTON MAN"

There was one man, who "lived, when he was to home," as he told me, "in the Red River Country," in the north-eastern part of Texas, having emigrated thither from Alabama, some years before. He was a tall, thin, awkward person, and wore a suit of clothes (probably bought "ready-made") which would have better suited a short, fat figure. Under his waistcoat he carried a large knife, with the hilt generally protruding at the breast. He had been with his family to his former home, for a business purpose, and was now returning to his plantation. His wife was a pale and harassed-looking woman; and he scarce ever paid her the smallest attention, not even sitting near her at the public table. Of his children, however, he seemed very fond; and they had a negro servant in attendance upon them, whom he was constantly scolding and threatening. Having been from home for six weeks, his impatience to return was very great, and was constantly aggravated by the frequent and long-continued stoppages of the boat. "Time's money, time's money!" he would be constantly saying, while we were taking on cotton—"time's worth more'n money to me now; a hundred per cent. more, 'cause I left my niggers all alone; not a dam white man within four mile on 'em."

I asked how many negroes he had.

"I've got twenty on 'em to home, and thar they ar! and thar they ar! and thar aint a dam soul of a white fellow within four mile on 'em."

"They are picking cotton, I suppose?"

"No, I got through pickin' 'fore I left."

"What work have they to do, then, now?"

"I set 'em to clairin', but they aint doin' a dam thing—not a dam thing, they aint; that's wat they are doin', that is—not a dam thing. I know that, as well as you do. That's the reason time's an object. I told the capting so, wen I came aboard: says I, 'capting,' says I, 'time is in the objective case with me.' No, sir, they aint doin' a dam solitary thing; that's what they are up to. I know that as well as anybody; I do. But I'll make it up, I'll make it up, when I get thar, now you'd better believe."

Once, when a lot of cotton, baled with unusual neatness, was coming on board, and some doubt had been expressed as to the economy of the method of baling, he said very loudly:

"Well, now, I'd be willin' to bet my salvation, that them thar's the heaviest bales that's come on to this boat."

"I'll bet you a hundred dollars of it," answered one.

"Well, if I was in the habit of bettin', I'd do it. I aint a bettin' man. But I am a cotton man, I am, and I don't car who knows it. I know cotton, I do. I'm dam if I know anythin' but cotton. I ought to know cotton, I had. I've been at it ever sin' I was a chile."

27. A CREW OF SLAVES AND IRISHMEN

The crew of the boat, as I have intimated, was composed partly of Irishmen, and partly of negroes; the latter were slaves, and were hired of their owners at $40 a month—the same wages paid to the Irishmen. A dollar of their wages was given to the negroes themselves, for each Sunday they were on the passage. So far as convenient, they were kept at work separately from the white hands; they were also messed separately. On Sunday I observed them dining in a group, on the cotton-bales. The food which was given to them in tubs, from the kitchen, was various and abundant, consisting of bean-porridge, bacon, corn-bread, ship's biscuit, potatoes, duff (pudding), and gravy. There was one knife used only, among ten of them; the bacon was cut and torn into shares; splinters of the bone and of fire-wood were used for forks; the porridge was passed from one to another, and drank out of the tub; but though excessively dirty and beast-like in their appearance and manners, they were good-natured and jocose as usual.

"Heah! you Bill," said one to another, who was on a higher tier of cotton, "pass down de dessart. You! up dar on de hill; de dessart! Augh! don't you know what de dessart be? De duff, you fool."

"Does any of de gemmen want some o' dese potatum?" asked another; and no answer being given, he turned the tub full of potatoes overboard, without any hesitation. It was evident he had never had to think on one day how he should be able to live the next.

Whenever we landed at night or on Sunday, for wood or cotton, there would be many negroes come on board from the neighbouring plantations, to sell eggs to the steward.

Sunday was observed by the discontinuance of public gambling in the cabin, and in no other way. At midnight gambling was resumed, and during the whole passage was never at any other time discontinued, night or day, so far as I saw. There were three men that seemed to be professional sharpers, and who probably played into each other's hands. One young man lost all the money he had with him—several hundred dollars.

28. MOBILE

Mobile, in its central, business part, is very compactly built, dirty and noisy, with little elegance, or evidence of taste or public spirit, in its people. A small, central, open square—the only public ground that I saw—was used as a horse and hog pasture, and clothes-drying yard. Out of the busier quarter, there is a good deal of the appearance of a thriving New England village—almost all the dwelling-houses having plots of ground enclosed around them, planted with trees and shrubs. The finest trees are the magnolia and live oak; and the most valuable shrub is the Cherokee rose, which is much used for hedges and screens. . . .

The Battle House, kept by Boston men, with Irish servants, I found an excellent hotel; but with higher charge than I had ever paid before. Prices, generally, in Mobile, range very high. There are large numbers of foreign merchants in the population; but a great deficiency of tradesmen and mechanics. . . .

The great business of the town is the transfer of cotton, from the producer to the manufacturer, from the waggon and the steamboat to the sea-going ship. Like all the other cotton-ports, Mobile labours under the disadvantage of a shallow harbour. At the wharves, there were only a few small craft and steamboats. All large sea-going vessels lie some thirty miles below, and their freights are transhipped in lighters [barges].

There appears to be a good deal of wealth and luxury, as well as senseless extravagance in the town. English merchants affect the character of the society, considerably; some very favourably—some, very much otherwise.

Chapter 3

Louisiana

Olmsted moved on to New Orleans from Mobile in mid-February 1853, in one of the more eventful legs of his journey (see map, page 11). He was quite taken with the South's largest and most diverse city, and he devoted more pages to it than to any other urban center he visited. Like many other outsiders, Olmsted was intrigued by New Orleans's unique racial order, and he followed his description of its distinctive society with more general reflections on the supposed licentiousness of the South as a whole, a topic that had become increasingly central in northern critiques of slavery and slaveholders.

After several days in New Orleans, Olmsted traveled up the Mississippi River and on to the Red River, which carried him into Louisiana's central and then northwestern region, where he made the town of Natchitoches his final destination. Along the way, he took advantage of visits to large sugar and cotton plantations—referring to the latter as the most profitable operation he had seen—to fully expound on the workings of both, including further insights into slave life and culture and how they varied from what he had observed in the Southeast. It was also in Louisiana that he first gave serious attention to small farmers and even poor whites, topics that would become more central to his observations and analysis from that point on.

Louisiana was the only state that factored into all three of Olmsted's journeys and all three of the volumes chronicling those trips. In condensing those books into The Cotton Kingdom, *he performed a chronological sleight of hand by subtly shifting his narrative from his first trip to his second (when accompanied by his brother). As he began to describe his trip up the Red River (Selection 38), he alerted readers to that transition in a single sentence: "I shall draw . . . upon a record of experience extending through nearly twelve months, but obtained in different journeys and in two different years."*

29. BY BOAT AND TRAIN TO NEW ORLEANS

There were a large number of steerage passengers occupying the main deck, forward of the shaft. Many of them were Irish, late immigrants, but the large majority were slaves, going on to New Orleans to be sold, or moving with their masters to Texas. There was a fiddle or two among them, and they were very merry, dancing and singing. A few, however, refused to join in the amusement, and looked very disconsolate. A large proportion of them were boys and girls, under twenty years of age.

On the forecastle-deck there was a party of emigrants, moving with waggons. There were three men, a father and his two sons, or sons-in-law, with their families, including a dozen or more women and children. They had two waggons, covered with calico and bed-ticks, supported by hoops, in which they carried their furniture and stores, and in which they also slept at night, the women in one, and the men in the other. They had six horses, two mules, and two pair of cattle with them. I asked the old man why he had taken his cattle along with him, when he was going so far by sea, and found that he had informed himself accurately of what it would cost him to hire or buy cattle at Galveston; and that taking into account the probable delay he would experience in looking for them there, he had calculated that he could afford to pay the freight on them, to have them with him, to go on at once into the country on his arrival, rather than to sell them at Mobile.

"But," said he, "there was one thing I didn't cakulate on, and I don't understand it; the capting cherged me two dollars and a half for 'wherfage.' I don't know what that means, do you? I want to know, because I don't car' to be imposed upon by nobody. I payed it without sayin' a word, 'cause I never travelled on the water before; next time I do, I shall be more sassy." I asked where he was going. Didn't know much about it, he said, but reckoned he could find a place where there was a good range, and plenty of game. If 'twas as good a range (pasture) as 'twas to Alabama when he first came there, he'd be satisfied. After he'd got his family safe through acclimating this time, he reckoned he shouldn't move again. He had moved about a good deal in his life. . . . They should try to find some heavy timbered land—good land, and go to clearing; didn't calculate to make any crops the first year—didn't calculate on it, though perhaps they might if they had good luck. They had come from an eastern county of Alabama. Had sold out his farm for two dollars an acre; best land in the district was worth four; land was naturally kind of thin, and now 'twas pretty much all worn out there. He had moved first from North Carolina, with his father. They never made anything to sell but cotton; made corn for their own use. Never had any negroes; reckoned he'd done about as well as if he had had them; reckoned a little better on the whole. No, he should not work negroes in Texas. "Niggers is so kerless, and want so much lookin' arter; they is so monstrous lazy; they won't do no work, you know, less you are clus to 'em all the time, and I don't feel like it. I couldn't, at my time of life, begin a-using the lash; and you know they do have to take that, all on 'em—and a heap on't, sometimes."

"I don't know much about it; they don't have slaves where I live."

"Then you come from a Free State; well, they've talked some of makin' Alabamy a Free State."

"I didn't know that."

"O, yes, there was a good deal of talk one time, as if they was goin' to do it right off. O, yes; there was two or three of the States this way, one time, come pretty nigh freein' the niggers—lettin' 'em all go free."

"And what do you think of it?"

"Well, I'll tell you what I think on it; I'd like it if we could get rid on 'em to yonst [at once]. I wouldn't like to hev 'em freed, if they was gwine to hang round. They ought to get some country, and put 'em war they could be by themselves. It wouldn't do no good to free 'em, and let 'em hang round, because they is so monstrous lazy; if they hadn't got nobody to take keer on 'em, you see they wouldn't do nothin' but juss nat'rally laze round, and steal, and pilfer, and no man couldn't live, you see, war they was—if they was free, no man couldn't live. And then, I've two objections; that's one on 'em—no man couldn't live—and this ere's the other; Now suppose they was free; you see they'd all think themselves just as good as we; of course they would, if they was free. Now, just suppose you had a family of children: how would you like to hev a nigger feelin' just as good as a white man? how'd you like to hev a nigger steppin' up to your darter? Of course you wouldn't; and that's the reason I wouldn't like to hev 'em free; but I tell you, I don't think it's right to hev 'em slaves so; that's the fac—taant right to keep 'em as they is."

I was awakened, in the morning, by the loud ringing of a hand-bell, and, turning out of my berth, dressed by dim lamp-light. The waiters were serving coffee and collecting baggage; and, upon stepping out of the cabin, I found that the boat was made fast to a long wooden jetty, and the passengers were going ashore. A passage-ticket for New Orleans was handed me, as I crossed the gang-plank. There was a rail-track and a train of cars upon the wharf, but no locomotive; and I got my baggage checked, and walked on toward the shore.

It was early daylight—a fog rested on the water, and only the nearest point could be discerned. There were many small buildings near the jetty, erected on piles over the water—bathing-houses, bowling-alleys, and billiard-rooms, with other indications of a place of holiday resort—and, on reaching the shore, I found a slumbering village. . . . When a locomotive backed, screaming hoarsely, down the jetty . . . I returned to get my seat. . . .

Off we puffed [on the train] through the little village of white houses—whatever it was—and away into a dense, gray cypress forest. For three or four rods, each side of the track, the trees had all been felled and removed, leaving a dreary strip of swamp, covered with stumps. This was bounded and intersected by broad ditches, or narrow and shallow canals, with a great number of very small punts in them. So it continued, for two or three miles; then the ground became dryer, there was an abrupt termination of the gray wood; the fog was lifting and drifting off, in ragged, rosy clouds, disclosing a flat country, skirted still, and finally bounded, in the background, with the swamp-forest. A few low houses, one story high, all having verandahs before them, were scattered thinly over it.

At length, a broad road struck in by the side of the track; the houses became more frequent; soon forming a village street, with smoke ascending from breakfast fires; windows and doors opening, maids sweeping steps, bakers' waggons passing, and broad streets, little built upon, breaking off at right angles.

30. TOURING NEW ORLEANS

There was a sign, "*Café du Faubourg*," and, putting my head out of the window, I saw that we must have arrived at New Orleans. We reached the terminus, which was surrounded with *fiacres* [small carriages], in the style of Paris. "To the Hotel St. Charles," I said to a driver, confused with the loud French and quiet English of the crowd about me. "*Oui, yer 'onor*," was the reply of my Irish-born fellow-citizen: another passenger was got, and away we rattled through narrow dirty streets, among grimy old stuccoed walls; high arched windows and doors, balconies and entresols, and French noises and French smells, French signs, ten to one of English, but with funny polyglotic arrangements, sometimes, from which less influential families were not excluded. . . .

Now the signs became English, and the new brick buildings American. We turned into a broad street, in which shutters were being taken from great glass store-fronts, and clerks were exercising their ingenuity in the display of muslin, and silks, and shawls. In the middle of the broad street there was an open space of waste ground, looking as if the corporation had not been able to pave the whole of it at once, and had left this interval to be attended to when the treasury was better filled. Crossing through a gap in this waste, we entered a narrow street of high buildings, French, Spanish, and English signs, the latter predominating; and at the second block, I was landed before the great Grecian portico of the stupendous, tasteless, ill-contrived, and inconvenient St. Charles Hotel.

After a bath and breakfast, I returned, with great interest, to wander in the old French town, the characteristics of which I have sufficiently indicated. Among the houses, one occasionally sees a relic of ancient Spanish builders, while all the newer edifices have the characteristics of the dollar-pursuing Yankees.

. . .

First and last, I spent some weeks in New Orleans and its vicinity. I doubt if there is a city in the world, where the resident population has been so divided in its origin, or where there is such a variety in the tastes, habits, manners, and moral codes of the citizens. Although this injures civic enterprise — which the peculiar situation of the city greatly demands to be directed to means of cleanliness, convenience, comfort, and health — it also gives a greater scope to the working of individual enterprise, taste, genius, and conscience; so that nowhere are the higher qualities of man — as displayed in generosity, hospitality, benevolence, and courage — better developed, or the lower qualities, likening him to a beast, less interfered with, by law or the action of public opinion.

31. QUADROON SOCIETY

There is one, among the multitudinous classifications of society in New Orleans, which is a very peculiar and characteristic result of the prejudices, vices, and customs of the various elements of colour, class, and nation, which have been there brought together.

I refer to a class composed of the illegitimate offspring of white men and coloured women (mulattoes or quadroons), who, from habits of early life, the advantages of education, and the use of wealth, are too much superior to the negroes, in general, to associate with them, and are not allowed by law, or the popular prejudice, to marry white people. The girls are frequently sent to Paris to be educated, and are very accomplished. They are generally pretty, often handsome. I have rarely, if ever, met more beautiful women than one or two whom I saw by chance, in the streets. They are better formed, and have a more graceful and elegant carriage than Americans in general, while they seem to have commonly inherited or acquired much of the taste and skill, in the selection and arrangement, and the way of wearing dresses and ornaments, that is the especial distinction of the women of Paris. Their beauty and attractiveness being their fortune, they cultivate and cherish with diligence every charm or accomplishment they are possessed of.

Of course, men are attracted by them, associate with them, are captivated, and become attached to them, and, not being able to marry them legally, and with the usual forms and securities for constancy, make such arrangements "as can be agreed upon." When a man makes a declaration of love to a girl of this class, she will admit or deny, as the case may be, her happiness in receiving it; but, supposing she is favourably disposed, she will usually refer the applicant to her mother. The mother inquires, like the "Countess of Kew," into the circumstances of the suitor; ascertains whether he is able to maintain a family, and, if satisfied with him, in these and other respects, requires from him security that he will support her daughter in a style suitable to the habits in which she has been bred, and that, if he should ever leave her, he will give her a certain sum for her future support, and a certain additional sum for each of the children she shall then have.

The wealth, thus secured, will, of course, vary—as in society with higher assumptions of morality—with the value of the lady in the market; that is, with her attractiveness, and the number and value of other suitors she may have, or may reasonably expect. Of course, I do not mean that love has nothing at all to do with it; but love is sedulously restrained, and held firmly in hand, until the road of competency is seen to be clear, with less humbug than our English custom requires about it. Everything being satisfactorily arranged, a tenement in a certain quarter of the town is usually taken, and the couple move into it and go to housekeeping—living as if they were married. The woman is not, of course, to be wholly deprived of the society of others—her former acquaintances are continued, and she sustains her relations as daughter, sister, and friend. Of course, too, her husband (she calls him so) will be likely to continue, also, more or less in, and form a part of, this kind of society. There are parties and balls—*bals masqués*—and all the movements and customs of other fashionable society, which they can enjoy in it, if they wish. The women of this sort are represented to be exceedingly affectionate in disposition, and constant beyond reproach.

During all the time a man sustains this relation, he will commonly be moving, also, in reputable society on the other side of the town; not improbably, eventually he marries, and has a family establishment elsewhere. Before doing this, he may separate from his *placée* (so she is termed). If so, he pays her according to agreement, and as much more, perhaps, as his affection for her, or his sense of the cruelty of the proceeding, may lead him to; and she has the world before her again, in the position of a widow. Many men continue for a long time, to support both establishments—particularly if their legal marriage is one *de convenance* [of convenience]. But many others form so strong attachments, that the relation is never discontinued, but becomes, indeed, that of marriage, except that it is not legalized or solemnized. These men leave their estate, at death, to their children, to whom they may have previously given every advantage of education they could command. What becomes of the boys, I am not informed; the girls, sometimes, are removed to other countries, where their colour does not prevent their living reputable lives; but, of course, mainly continue in the same society, and are fated to a life similar to that of their mothers.

I have described this custom as it was described to me; I need hardly say, in only its best aspects. The crime and heart-breaking sorrow that must frequently result from it, must be evident to every reflective reader.

32. THE LICENTIOUS SOUTH

It is asserted by Southerners who have lived at the North, and Northerners who lived at the South, that although the facilities for licentiousness are much greater at the South, the evil of licentiousness is much greater at the North. Not because the average standard of "respectable position" requires a less expenditure at the South, for the contrary is the case.[1] But it is said licentiousness at the North is far more captivating, irresistible, and ruinous than at the South. Its very intrigues, cloaks, hazards, and expenses, instead of repressing the passions of young men, exasperate them, and increase its degrading effect upon their character, producing hypocrisy, interfering with high ambitions, destroying self-respect, causing the worst possible results to their health, and giving them habits which are inimical to future domestic contentment and virtue.

Possibly there is some ground for this assertion with regard to young men in towns, though in rural life the advantage of the North, I believe, is incomparable.

Mrs. Douglass, a Virginia woman, who was tried, convicted, and punished, a year or two since, for teaching a number of slaves to read, contrary to law, says in a letter from her jail—

[1] [Olmsted] A gentleman in an inland Southern town said to me, "I have now but one servant; if I should marry, I should be obliged to buy three more, and that alone would withdraw from my capital at least three thousand dollars."

This subject demands the attention, not only of the religious population, but of statesmen and law-makers. It is one great evil hanging over the Southern Slave States, destroying domestic happiness and the peace of thousands. It is summed up in the single word—*amalgamation*. This, and this only, causes the vast extent of ignorance, degradation, and crime that lies like a black cloud over the whole South. And the practice is more general than even the Southerners are willing to allow.

Neither is it to be found only in the lower order of the white population. It pervades the entire society. Its followers are to be found among all ranks, occupations, and professions. The white mothers and daughters of the South have suffered under it for years—have seen their dearest affections trampled upon—their hopes of domestic happiness destroyed, and their future lives embittered, even to agony, by those who should be all in all to them, as husbands, sons, and brothers. I cannot use too strong language in reference to this subject, for I know that it will meet with a heartfelt response from every Southern woman.

A negress was hung this year in Alabama, for the murder of her child. At her trial she confessed her guilt. She said her owner was the father of the child, and that her mistress knew it, and treated it so cruelly in consequence, that she had killed it to save it from further suffering, and also to remove a provocation to her own ill-treatment.

A large planter told, as a reason for sending his boys to the North to be educated, that there was no possibility of their being brought up in decency at home. Another planter told me that he was intending to move to a free country on this account. He said that the practice was not occasional or general, it was universal. "There is not," he said, "a likely-looking black girl in this State that is not the concubine of a white man. There is not an old plantation in which the grandchildren of the owner are not whipped in the field by his overseer. I cannot bear that the blood of the—— should run in the veins of slaves." He was of an old Scotch family. . . .

33. VISIT TO A SUGAR PLANTATION

[*St Charles Parish, La.*]—I came to Mr. R.'s[1] plantation by a steamboat, late at night. As the boat approached the shore, near his house, her big bell having been rung some ten minutes previously, a negro came out

---

[1] Mr. R. was Richard Taylor, a prominent sugar planter who was the only son of President Zachary Taylor. He is the subject of a full biography by T. Michael Parrish (see Selected Bibliography).

with a lantern to meet her. The boat's bow was run boldly against the bank; I leaped ashore, the clerk threw out a newspaper and a package, saying to the negro, "That's for your master, and that's for so-and-so, tell your master, and ask him to give it to him." The boat bounded off at once, by her own elasticity, the starboard wheel was backed for a turn or two, and the next minute the great edifice was driving up the stream again—not a rope having been lifted, nor any other movement having been made on board, except by the pilot and engineer.

"Do you belong to Mr. R.?" I asked the negro. "Yes, sir; is you going to our house, master?" "Yes." "I'll show you the way, then, sir"; and he conducted me in, leaving the parcels the clerk had thrown out, where they had fallen, on the bank....

Mr. R. is a Southerner by birth, but was educated at the North, where, also, and in foreign countries, he has spent a large part of his life. He is a man of more than usual precision of mind, energetic and humane; and while his negroes seemed to be better disciplined than any others I had seen, they evidently regarded him with affection, respect, and pride.

He had been ill for some weeks previous to my visit, and when he walked out with me, on the second day, it was the first time since the commencement of his illness that his field-hands had seen him.

The first negroes we met were half a dozen women, who were going up to the nursery to suckle their children—the overseer's bell having been just rung (at eleven o'clock), to call them in from work for that purpose. Mr. R. said that he allowed them two hours to be with their children while nursing at noon, and to leave work an hour earlier at night than the other field-hands. The women all stopped as we met them, and asked, with much animation:

"Oh, master! how is 'ou?"

"Well, I'm getting up. How are you, girls?"

"Oh, we's well, sir."

"The children all well?"

"Yes, master, all but Sukey's, sir."

"Sukey's? What, isn't that well yet?"

"No, master."

"But it's getting well, is it not?"

"Yes, master."

Soon after we met a boy, driving a cart. He pulled up as he came against us, and, taking off his hat, asked, "How is 'ou, master?"

"I'm getting well, you see. If I don't get about, and look after you, I'm afraid we shan't have much of a crop, I don't know what you niggers will do for Christmas money."

"Ha!—look heah, massa!—you jus' go right straight on de ways you's goin'; see suthin' make you laugh, ha! ha!" (meaning the work that had been done while he was ill, and the good promise of a crop).

The plantation contained about nine hundred acres of tillage land, and a large tract of "swamp," or woodland, was attached to it. The tillage land was inclosed all in one field by a strong cypress post and rail fence, and was drained by two canals, five feet deep, running about twenty feet apart, and parallel—the earth from both being thrown together, so as to make a high, dry road between them, straight through the middle of the plantation.

Fronting upon the river, and but six or eight rods from the public road, which everywhere runs close along the shore inside the levee, was the mansion of the proprietor: an old Creole house, the lower story of brick and the second of wood, with a broad gallery, shaded by the extended roof, running all around it; the roof steep, and shedding water on four sides, with ornaments of turned wood where lines met, and broken by several small dormer windows. The gallery was supported by round brick columns, and arches. The parlours, library, and sleeping rooms of the white family were all on the second floor. Between the house and the street was a yard, planted formally with orange-trees and other evergreens. A little on one side of the house stood a large two-story, square dove-cot [structure housing domestic pigeons], which is a universal appendage of a sugar-planter's house. In the rear of the house was another large yard, in which, irregularly placed, were houses for the family servants, a kitchen, stable, carriage-house, smoke-house, etc. Behind this rear-yard there was a vegetable garden, of an acre or more, in the charge of a negro gardener; a line of fig-trees were planted along the fence, but all the ground inclosed was intended to be cropped with vegetables for the family, and for the supply of "the people." I was pleased to notice, however, that the negro gardener had, of his own accord, planted some violets and other flowering plants. From a corner of the court a road ran to the sugar-works and the negro settlement, which were five or six hundred yards from the house.

The negro houses were exactly like those I have described on the Georgia Rice Plantation,[2] except that they were provided with broad galleries in front. They were as neat and well-made externally as the cottages usually provided by large manufacturing companies in New England,

---

[2] See Selection 16.

to be rented to their workmen. The clothing furnished the negroes, and the rations of bacon and meal, were the same as on other good plantations. During the grinding season extra rations of flour were served, and hot coffee was kept constantly in the sugar-house, and the hands on duty were allowed to drink it almost *ad libitum*. They were also allowed to drink freely of the hot *sirop*, of which they were extremely fond. A generous allowance of *sirop*, or molasses, was also given out to them, with their other rations, every week during the winter and early summer. In extremely hot weather it was thought to be unfavourable to health, and was discontinued. Rations of tobacco were also served. At Christmas, a sum of money, equal to one dollar for each hogshead of sugar made on the plantation, was divided among the negroes. The last year this had amounted to over two dollars a head. It was usually given to the heads of families. If any had been particularly careless or lazy, it was remembered at this Christmas dole. Of course, the effect of this arrangement, small as was the amount received by each person, was to give the labourers a direct interest in the economical direction of their labour: the advantage of it was said to be evident.

Mr. R. had purchased the plantation but three years before, and had afterwards somewhat increased its area by buying out several poor people, who had owned small farms adjoining. He had greatly extended and improved the drainage, and had nearly doubled the force of negroes employed upon it, adding to the number that he purchased with the land, nearly as many more whom he had inherited, and whom he transferred to it from an old cotton plantation that he had formerly lived upon.

He had considerably more than doubled the stock of mules and oxen; had built entirely new cabins for all the negroes, and new sugar-works and stables. His whole capital, he said, when he first bought the plantation, would not have paid half the price of it and of the cost of stocking it as he had done. Most men when they buy a plantation, he informed me, go very heavily in debt; frequently the purchase is made three quarters on credit.

34. THE ECONOMY OF SUGAR

"Buying a plantation," were [Mr. R.'s] words, "whether a sugar or cotton plantation, in this country, is usually essentially a gambling operation. The capital invested in a sugar plantation of the size of mine ought not to be less than $150,000. The purchaser pays down what he can, and usually gives security for the payment of the balance in six annual installments, with interest (10 per cent. per annum) from the date of the purchase. Success in sugar, as well as cotton planting, is dependent on so many circumstances, that it is as much trusting to luck as betting on a throw of dice. If his first crop proves a bad one, he must borrow money of the Jews in New Orleans to pay his first note; they will sell him this on the best terms they can—often at not less than 25 per cent. per annum. If three or four bad crops follow one another, he is ruined. But this is seldom the case, and he lives on, one year gaining a little on his debts, but almost as often enlarging them. Three or four years ago there was hardly a planter in Louisiana or Mississippi who was not in very embarrassed circumstances, nearly every one having his crops pledged to his creditors long before they were secured. The good prices and good crops of the last few years have set them all on their legs again; and this year all the jewellers' shops, and stores of rich furniture and dry goods, in New Orleans, were cleared out by the middle of the season, and everybody feels strong and cheerful. I have myself been particularly fortunate; I have made three good crops in succession. Last year I made six hundred and fifty hogsheads of sugar, and twelve hundred barrels of molasses. The molasses alone brought me a sum sufficient to pay all my plantation expenses; and the sugar yields me a clear profit of twenty-five per cent. on my whole investment. If I make another crop this year as good as that, I shall be able to discount my outstanding notes, and shall be clear of debt at the end of four years, instead of six, which was all I had hoped for." . . .

Mr. R. modestly credited his extraordinary success to "luck"; but I was satisfied, upon examining his improvements, and considering the reasons, which he readily gave for every operation which he showed, or described to me, that intelligence, study, and enterprise had seldom better claims to reward. Adjoining his plantation there was another of nearly twice the size, on which an equal number of negroes and only half the number of cattle were employed; and the proprietor, I was told, had had rather *bad luck*: he had, in fact, made but little more than half as much sugar as Mr. R. I inquired of the latter if there was any advantage in his soil over that of his neighbour's. "I think not," he replied; "my best cane was made on a piece of land adjoining his, which, before I bought it, was thought unfit for cultivation. The great advantage I had over him last year, mainly arose from my having secured a more complete drainage of all my land." . . .

The sugar-cane is a perennial-rooted plant, and the stalk does not attain its full size, under favourable circumstances, in less growing time than twelve months; and seed does not usually form upon it until the thirteenth or fourteenth month. This function (termed *arrowing*) it only performs in a very hot and steadily hot climate, somewhat rarely even in the West Indies. The plant is, at all stages, extremely susceptible to cold, a moderate frost not only suspending its growth, but disorganizing it so that the chemical qualities of its sap are changed, and it is rendered valueless for sugar making.

As frosts of considerable severity are common in all parts of Louisiana, during three months of the year, of course the sugarcane is there never permitted to attain its full growth. To so much greater perfection does it arrive in the West Indies, that the cane produced on one acre will yield from 3,000 to 6,000 lbs. of sugar, while in Louisiana 1,000 is considered the average obtained. "I could make sugar in the climate of Cuba," said a Louisiana planter to me, "for half the price that, under the most favourable circumstances, it must cost here." . . .

I must confess that there seems to me room for grave doubt if the capital, labour, and especially the human life, which have been and which continue to be spent in converting the swamps of Louisiana into sugar plantations, and in defending them against the annual assaults of the river, and the fever and the cholera, could not have been better employed somewhere else. It is claimed as a great advantage of Slavery . . . that what has been done for this purpose never would have been done without it. . . . There is now great wealth in Louisiana; but I question if greater wealth would not have been obtained by the same expenditure of human labour, and happiness, and life, in very many other directions.

35. SLAVES AND THE "GRINDING-SEASON"

The grinding-season is the harvest of the sugar-planter; it commences in October, and continues for two or three months, during which time, the greatest possible activity and the utmost labour of which the hands are capable, are required to secure the product of the previous labour of the year. Mr. R. assured me that during the last grinding-season nearly every man, woman, and child on his plantation, including the overseer and himself, were on duty fully eighteen hours a day. From the moment grinding first commences, until the end of the season, it is never discontinued: the fires under the boiler never go out, and the negroes only rest for six hours in the twenty-four, by relays—three-quarters of them being constantly at work.

Notwithstanding the severity of the labour required of them at this time, Mr. R. said that his negroes were as glad as he was himself to have the time for grinding arrive, and they worked with greater cheerfulness than at any other season. How can those persons who are always so ready to maintain that the slaves work less than free labourers in free countries, and that for that reason they are to be envied by them, account for this? That at Mr. R.'s plantation it was the case that the slaves enjoyed most that season of the year when the hardest labour was required of them, I have, in addition to Mr. R.'s own evidence, good reason to believe, which I shall presently report. And the reason of it evidently is, that they are then better paid; they have better and more varied food and stimulants than usual, but especially they have a degree of freedom, and of social pleasure, and a variety of occupation which brings a recreation of the mind, and to a certain degree gives them strength for, and pleasure in, their labour. Men of sense have discovered that when they desire to get extraordinary exertions from their slaves, it is better to offer them rewards than to whip them; to encourage them, rather than to drive them.

36. POOR WHITE NEIGHBORS

At one corner of Mr. R.'s plantation, there was a hamlet consisting of about a dozen small houses or huts, built of wood or clay, in the old French peasant style. The residents owned small farms, on which they raised a little corn and rice; but Mr. R. described them as lazy vagabonds, doing but little work, and spending much time in shooting, fishing, and play. He wanted much to buy all their land, and get them to move away. He had already bought out some of them, and had made arrangements by which he hoped soon to get hold of the land of some of the rest. He was willing to pay two or three times as much as the property was actually worth, to get them to move off. As fast as he got possession, he destroyed their houses and gardens, removed their fences and trees, and brought all their land into his cane-plantation.

Some of them were mechanics. One was a very good mason, and he employed him in building his sugar-works and refinery; but he would be glad to get rid of them all, and depend entirely on slave mechanics—of these he had several already, and he could buy more when he needed them.

Why did he [Mr. R.] so dislike to have these poor people living near him, I asked? Because, he straightway answered, they demoralized his negroes. Seeing them living in apparent comfort, without much property and without steady labour, the slaves could not help thinking that it was unnecessary for men to work so hard as they themselves were obliged to, and that if they were free they would not work. Besides, the intercourse of these people with the negroes was not favourable to good discipline. They would get the negroes to do them little services, and would pay with luxuries which he did not wish his slaves to have. It was better that they never saw anybody off their own plantation; they should, if possible, have no intercourse with any other white men than their owner or overseer; especially, it was desirable that they should not see white men who did not command their respect, and whom they did not always feel to be superior to themselves, and able to command them.

The nuisance of petty traders dealing with the negroes, and encouraging them to pilfer, which I found everywhere a great annoyance to planters, seems to be greater on the banks of the Mississippi than elsewhere. The traders generally come on boats, which they moor at night on the shore, adjoining the negro-quarters, and float away whenever they have obtained any booty, with very small chance of detection. One day, during my visit at Mr. R.'s, a neighbour called to apprise him that one of these trading-boats was in the vicinity, that he might take precautions to prevent his negroes dealing with it. "The law," he observed, with much feeling, "is entirely inadequate to protect us against these rascals; it rather protects them than us. They easily evade detection in breaking it; and we can never get them punished, except we go beyond or against the law ourselves." . . . Mr. R. said that he had lately caught one of his own negroes going towards one of the "chicken-thieves" (so the traders' boats are locally called) with a piece of machinery, unscrewed from his sugar-works, which had cost him eighty dollars, but which would, very likely, have been sold for a drink. If the negro had succeeded in reaching the boat, as he would, if a watch had not been kept, he could never have recovered it. There would have been no witnesses to the sale; the stolen goods would have been hid on board until the boat reached New Orleans; or, if an officer came to search the boat, they would have been dropped into the river, before he got on board.

This neighbour of Mr. R.'s had been educated in France. Conversing on the inconveniences of Slavery, he acknowledged that it was not only an uneconomical system, but a morally wrong one; "but," he said, "it was not instituted by us—we are not responsible for it. It is unfortunately fixed upon us; we could not do away with it if we wished; our duty is only to make the best of a bad thing; to lessen its evils as much as we can, so far as we have to do with it individually."

Mr. R. himself also acknowledged Slavery to be a very great evil, morally and economically. It was a curse upon the South; he had no doubt at all about it: nothing would be more desirable than its removal, if it were possible to be accomplished. But he did not think it could be abolished without instituting greater evils than those sought to be remedied. Its influence on the character of the whites was what was most deplorable. He was sorry to think that his children would have to be subject to it. He thought that eventually, if he were able to afford it, he should free his slaves and send them to Africa.

37. CONVERSATION WITH WILLIAM, A SLAVE

When I left Mr. R.'s, I was driven about twenty miles in a buggy, by one of his house servants. He was inclined to be talkative and communicative; and as he expressed great affection and respect for his owner, I felt at liberty to question him on some points upon which I had always previously avoided conversing with slaves. . . .

He first said that he supposed that I would see that he was not a "Creole nigger"; he came from Virginia. He reckoned the Virginia negroes were better looking than those who were raised here; there were no black people anywhere in the world who were so "well made" as those who were born in Virginia. He asked if I lived in New Orleans; and where? I told him that I lived at the North. He asked:

"Da's a great many brack folks dah, massa?"

"No; very few."

"Da's a great many in Virginny; more'n da is heah?"

"But I came from beyond Virginia — from New York."

He had heard there were a great many black folk in New York. I said there were a good many in the city; but few in the country. Did I live in the country? What people did I have for servants? Thought, if I hired all my labour, it must be very dear. He inquired further about negroes there. I told him they were all free, and described their general condition; told him what led them to congregate in cities, and what the effect was. He said the negroes, both slave and free, who lived in New Orleans, were better off than those who lived in the country. Why? Because they make more money, and it is "gayer" there, and there is more "society." He then drew a contrast between Virginia, as he recollected it, and Louisiana. There is but one road in this country. In Virginia, there are roads running in every direction, and often crossing each other. You could see so much more "society," and there was so much more "variety" than here. He would not like now to go back to Virginia to live, because he had got used to this country, and had all his acquaintances here, and knew the ways of the people. He could speak French. He would like to go to New Orleans, though; would rather live in New Orleans than any other place in the world.

After a silence of some minutes, he said, abruptly —

"If I was free, I would go to Virginia, and see my old mudder." He had left her when he was thirteen years old. He reckoned he was now thirty-three. "I don't well know, dough, exactly, how old I is; but, I rec'lect, de day I was taken away, my ole mudder she tell me I was tirteen year old." He did not like to come away at all; he "felt dreadful bad"; but, now he was used to it, he liked living here. He came across the Blue Ridge, and he recollected that, when he first saw it, he thought it was a dark piece of sky, and he wondered what it would be like when they came close to it. He was brought, with a great many other negroes, in waggons, to Louisville; and then they were put on board a steamboat, and brought down here. He was sold, and put on this plantation, and had been on it ever since. He had been twice sold, along with it. Folks didn't very often sell their servants away here, as they did in Virginia. They were selling their servants, in Virginia, all the time; but, here, they did not very often sell them, except they run away. When a man would run away, and they could not do anything with him, they always sold him off. The people were almost all French. "Were there any French in New York?" he asked. I told him there were; but not as many as in Louisiana. "I s'pose dah is more of French people in Lusiana, dan dah is anywhar else in all de world — a'nt dah, massa?"

"Except in France."

"Wa's dat, sar?"

"France is the country where all the Frenchmen came from, in the first place."

"Wa's dat France, massa?"

"France is a country across the ocean, the big water, beyond Virginia, where all the Frenchmen first came from; just as the black people all came first from Africa, you know."

"I've heered, massa, dat dey sell one anoder dah, in de fus place. Does you know, sar, was dat so?" This was said very gravely.

I explained the savage custom of making slaves of prisoners of war, and described the constant wars of the native Africans. I told him that they were better off here than they would be to be the slaves of cruel savages, in Africa. He turned, and looking me anxiously in the face, like a child, asked:

"*Is* de brack folks better off to be here, massa?"

I answered that I thought so; and described the heathenish barbarism of the people of Africa. I made exception of Liberia,[1] knowing that his master thought of some time sending him there, and described it as a place that was settled by negroes who went back there from this country. He said he had heard of it, and that they had sent a good many free negroes from New Orleans there.

After a moment's pause, he inquired—very gravely, again:

"*Why is it*, massa, when de brack people is free, dey wants to send 'em away out of dis country?"

The question took me aback. After bungling a little—for I did not like to tell him the white people were afraid to have them stay here—I said that it was thought to be a better place for them there. He replied, he should think, that, when they had got used to this country, it was much better that they should be allowed to stay here. He would not like to go out of this country. He wouldn't like even to go to Virginia now, though Virginia was such a pleasant country; he had been here so long, seemed like this was the best place for him to live. To avoid discussion of the point, I asked what he would do, if he were free?

"If I was free, massa; *if I was free*" (with great animation), "I would—well, sar, de fus thing I would do, if I was free, I would go to work for a year, and get some money for myself,—den—den—den, massa, dis is what I do—I buy me, fus place, a little house, and little lot land, and den—no; den—den—I would go to old Virginny, and see my old mudder. Yes, sar, I would like to do dat fus thing; den, when I com back, de fus thing I'd do, I'd get me a wife; den, I'd take her to my house, and I would live with her dar; and I would raise things in my garden, and take 'em to New Orleans, and sell I 'em dar, in de market. Dat's de way I would live, if I was free."

He said, in answer to further inquiries, that there were many free negroes all about this region. Some were very rich. He pointed out to me three plantations, within twenty miles, owned by coloured men. These bought black folks, he said, and had servants of their own. They were very bad masters, very hard and cruel—hadn't any feeling. "You might think, master, dat dey would be good to dar own nation; but dey

[1] See Selection 9, note 1.

is not. I will tell you de truth, massa; I know I'se got to answer; and it's a fact, dey is very bad masters, sar. I'd rather be a servant to any man in de world, dan to a brack man. If I was sold to a brack man, I'd drown myself. I would dat—I'd drown myself! dough I shouldn't like to do dat nudder; but I wouldn't be sold to a coloured master for anyting."

If he had got to be sold, he would like best to have an American master buy him. The French people did not clothe their servants well; though now they did much better than when he first came to Louisiana. The French masters were very severe, and "dey whip dar niggers most to deff—dey whip de flesh off of 'em."

Nor did they feed them as well as the Americans. "Why, sometimes, massa, dey only gives 'em dry corn—don't give out no meat at all." I told him this could not be so, for the law required that every master would serve out meat to his negroes. "Oh, but some on 'em don't mind Law, if he does say so, massa. Law never here; don't know anything about him. *Very often*, dey only gives 'em dry corn—I knows dat; I sees de niggers. Didn't you see de niggers on our plantation, sar? Well, you nebber see such a good-looking lot of niggers as ours on any of de French plantations, did you, massa? Why, dey all looks fat, and dey's all got good clothes, and dey look as if dey all had plenty to eat, and hadn't got no work to do, ha! ha! ha! Don't dey? But dey does work, dough. Dey does a heap o' work. But dey don't work so hard as dey does on some ob de French plantations. Oh, dey does work *too* hard on dem, sometimes."

"You work hard in the grinding season, don't you?"

"O yes; den we works hard; we has to work hard den: harder an any oder time of year. But, I tell 'ou, massa, I likes to hab de grinding season come; yes, I does—rader dan any oder time of year, dough we work so hard den. I wish it was grinding season all de year roun'—only Sundays."

"Why?"

"Because—oh, because it's merry and lively. All de brack people like it when we begin to grind."

"You have to keep grinding Sundays?"

"Yes, can't stop, when we begin to grind, till we get tru."

"You don't often work Sundays, except then?"

"No, massa! nebber works Sundays, except when der crap's weedy, and we want to get tru 'fore rain comes; den, wen we work Sunday, massa gives us some oder day for holiday—Monday, if we get tru." . . .

He again recurred to the fortunate condition of the negroes on his master's plantation. He thought it was the best plantation in the State, and he did not believe there was a better lot of negroes in the State;

some few of them, whom his master had brought from his former plantation, were old; but altogether, they were "as right good a lot of niggers" as could be found anywhere. They could do all the work that was necessary to be done on the plantation. On some old plantations they had not nearly as many negroes as they needed to make the crop, and they "drove 'em awful hard"; but it wasn't so on his master's: they could do all the work, and do it well, and it was the best worked plantation, and made the most sugar to the hand of any plantation he knew of. All the niggers had enough to eat, and were well clothed; their quarters were good, and they got a good many presents. He was going on enthusiastically, when I asked:

"Well, now, wouldn't you rather live on such a plantation than to be free, William?"

"Oh! no, sir, I'd rather be free! Oh, yes, sir, I'd like it better to be free; I would dat, master."

"Why would you?"

"Why, you see, master, if I was free—if I was *free*, I'd have all my time to myself. I'd rather work for myself. Yes. I'd like dat better."

"But then, you know, you'd have to take care of yourself, and you'd get poor."

"No, sir, I would not get poor, I would get rich; for you see, master, then I'd work all the time for myself."

"Suppose all the black people on your plantation, or all the black people in the country were made free at once, what do you think would become of them?—what would they do, do you think? You don't suppose there would be much sugar raised, do you?"

"Why, yes, master, I do. Why not, sir? What would de brack people do? Wouldn't dey hab to work for dar libben? and de wite people own all de land—war dey goin' to work? Dey hire demself right out again, and work all de same as before. And den, wen dey work for demself, dey work harder dan dey do now to get more wages—a heap harder. I tink so, sir. I would do so, sir. I would work for hire. I don't own any land; I hab to work right away again for massa, to get some money."

Perceiving from the readiness of these answers that the subject had been a familiar one with him, I immediately asked: "The black people talk among themselves about this, do they; and they think so generally?"

"Oh! yes, sir; dey talk so; dat's wat dey tink."

"Then they talk about being free a good deal, do they?"

"Yes, sir. Dey—dat is, dey say dey wish it was so; dat's all dey talk, master—dat's all, sir."

His caution was evidently excited, and I inquired no further.

38. UP THE RED RIVER

The largest part of the cotton crop of the United States is now produced in the Mississippi valley, including the lands contiguous to its great Southern tributary streams, the Red River and others. The proportion of the whole crop which is produced in this region is constantly and very rapidly increasing. This increase is chiefly gained by the forming of new plantations and the transfer of slave-labour westward. The common planter of this region lives very differently to those whose plantations I have hitherto described. What a very different person he is, and what a very different thing his plantation is from the class usually visited by travellers in the South, I learned by an extended experience. I presume myself to have been ordinarily well-informed when I started from home, but up to this point in my first journey had no correct idea of the condition and character of the common cotton-planters. I use the word common in reference to the whole region: there are some small districts in which the common planter is a rich man—really rich. But over the whole district there are comparatively few of these, and . . . I shall show what the many are—as I found them. I shall draw for this purpose upon a record of experience extending through nearly twelve months, but obtained in different journeys and in two different years.

My first observation of the common cotton-planters was had on the steamboat, between Montgomery and Mobile, and has already been described.[1] My second experience among them was on a steam-boat bound up the Red River.

On a certain Saturday morning, when I had determined upon the trip, I found that two boats, the Swamp Fox and the St. Charles, were advertised to leave the same evening, for the Red River. I went to the levee, and, finding the St. Charles to be the better of the two, I asked her clerk if I could engage a state-room. . . .

The St. Charles was crowded with passengers, and her decks were piled high with freight. Bumboatmen [peddlers in small boats], about the bows, were offering shells, and oranges, and bananas; and news-boys, and peddlers, and tract distributors, were squeezing about with their wares among the passengers. I had confidence in their instinct; there had been no such numbers of them the previous evenings, and I made up my mind, although past seven o'clock, that the St. Charles would not let her fires go down again.

[1] See Selection 25.

39. ENCOUNTERS WITH *UNCLE TOM'S CABIN*

Among the peddlers there were two of "cheap literature," and among their yellow covers, each had two or three copies of the cheap edition (pamphlet) of "Uncle Tom's Cabin."[1] They did not cry it out as they did the other books they had, but held it forth among others, so its title could be seen. One of them told me he carried it because gentlemen often inquired for it, and he sold a good many; at least three copies were sold to passengers on the boat. Another young man, who looked like a beneficiary of the Education Society, endeavouring to pass a college vacation in a useful and profitable manner, was peddling a Bible Defence of Slavery, which he made eloquent appeals, in the manner of a pastoral visit, to us, each personally, to purchase. He said it was prepared by a clergyman of Kentucky, and every slaveholder ought to possess it. When he came to me, I told him that I owned no slaves, and therefore had no occasion for it. He answered that the world was before me, and I perhaps yet might own many of them. I replied so decidedly that I should not, that he appeared to be satisfied that my conscience would not need the book, and turned back again to a man sitting beside me, who had before refused to look at it. He now urged again that he should do so, and forced it into his hands, open at the title-page, on which was a vignette, representing a circle of coloured gentlemen and ladies, sitting around a fire-place with a white person standing behind them, like a servant, reading from a book. "Here we see the African race as it is in America, under the blessed—"

"Now you go to hell! I've told you three times I didn't want your book. If you bring it here again I'll throw it overboard. I own niggers; and I calculate to own more of 'em, if I can get 'em, but I don't want any damn'd preachin' about it."

That was the last I saw of the book-peddler.

. . .

On the third day, just after the dinner-bell had rung, and most of the passengers had gone into the cabin, I was sitting alone on the gallery, reading a pamphlet, when a well-dressed middle-aged man accosted me.

[1] Harriet Beecher Stowe's *Uncle Tom's Cabin* was published in March 1852, less than a year prior to this encounter, and it quickly became the best-selling book ever published in the United States. Southerners bought far more copies than most were willing to acknowledge, even as they vehemently protested Stowe's portrait of their "peculiar institution."

"Is that the book they call Uncle Tom's Cabin, you are reading, sir?"

"No, sir."

"I did not know but it was; I see that there are two or three gentlemen on board that have got it. I suppose I might have got it in New Orleans: I wish I had. Have you ever seen it, sir?"

"Yes, sir."

"I'm told it shows up Slavery in very high colours."

"Yes, sir, it shows the evils of Slavery very strongly."

He took a chair near me, and said that, if it represented extreme cases as if they were general, it was not fair.

Perceiving that he was disposed to discuss the matter, I said that I was a Northern man, and perhaps not well able to judge; but that I thought that a certain degree of cruelty was necessary to make slave-labour generally profitable, and that not many were disposed to be more severe than they thought necessary. I believed there was little wanton cruelty. He answered, that Northern men were much mistaken in supposing that slaves were generally ill-treated. He was a merchant, but he owned a plantation, and he just wished I could see his negroes. "Why, sir," he continued, "my niggers' children all go regularly to a Sunday-school, just the same as my own, and learn verses, and catechism, and hymns. Every one of my grown-up niggers are pious, every one of them, and members of the church. I've got an old man that can pray—well, sir, I only wish I had as good a gift at praying! I wish you could just hear him pray. There are cases in which niggers are badly used; but they are not common. There are brutes everywhere. You have men, at the North, who whip their wives—and they kill them sometimes."

"Certainly, we have, sir; there are plenty of brutes at the North; but our law, you must remember, does not compel women to submit themselves to their power. A wife, cruelly treated, can escape from her husband, and can compel him to give her subsistence, and to cease from doing her harm. A woman could defend herself against her husband's cruelty, and the law would sustain her."

"It would not be safe to receive negroes' testimony against white people; they would be always plotting against their masters, if you did."

"Wives are not always plotting against their husbands."

"Husband and wife is a very different thing from master and slave."

"Your remark, that a bad man might whip his wife, suggested an analogy, sir."

"If the law was to forbid whipping altogether, the authority of the master would be at an end."

"And if you allow bad men to own slaves, and allow them to whip them, and deny the slave the privilege of resisting cruelty, do you not show that you think it is necessary to permit cruelty, in order to sustain the authority of masters, in general, over their slaves? That is, you establish cruelty as a necessity of Slavery—do you not?"

"No more than of marriage, because men may whip their wives cruelly."

"Excuse me, sir; the law does all it can, to prevent such cruelty between husband and wife; between master and slave it does not, because it cannot, without weakening the necessary authority of the master—that is, without destroying Slavery. It is, therefore, a fair argument against Slavery, to show how cruelly this necessity, of sustaining the authority of cruel and passionate men over their slaves, sometimes operates."

He asked what it was Uncle Tom "tried to make out."

I narrated the Red River episode,[2] and asked if such things could not possibly occur.

"Yes," replied he, "but very rarely. I don't know a man, in my parish, that could do such a thing. There are two men, though, in——, bad enough to do it, I believe; but it isn't a likely story, at all. In the first place, no coloured woman would be likely to offer any resistance, if a white man should want to seduce her."

After further conversation, he said, that a planter had been tried for injuring one of his negroes, at the court in his parish, the preceding summer. He had had a favourite, among his girls, and suspecting that she was unduly kind to one of his men, in an anger of jealousy he mutilated him. There was not sufficient testimony to convict him; "but," he said, "everybody believes he was guilty, and ought to have been punished. Nobody thinks there was any good reason for his being jealous of the boy."

I remarked that this story corroborated "Uncle Tom's Cabin"; it showed that it was all possible.

"Ah!" he answered, "but then nobody would have any respect for a man that treated his niggers cruelly."

I wondered, as I went in to dinner, and glanced at the long rows of surly faces, how many men there were there whose passions would be much restrained by the fear of losing the respect of their neighbours.

---

[2] The "Red River episode" is a reference to the latter part of Stowe's novel, in which Uncle Tom is sold to a particularly cruel and sadistic slaveholder, Simon Legree, whose mistreatment of Tom results in his death.

40. INSIDE A POOR COTTON FARM HOUSEHOLD

My original purpose had been to go high up [the] Red River at this time, but the long delay in the boat's leaving New Orleans, and her slow passage, obliged me to change my plans. . . .

We[1] spent several days in Natchitoches [a village on the Red River in Central Louisiana], purchasing horses and completing the preparations for our vagrant life in Texas.

One mild day of our stay we made a trip of some ten or fifteen miles out and back, at the invitation of a planter, whose acquaintance we had made at the hotel. We started in good season, but were not long in losing our way and getting upon obscure roads through the woods. The planter's residence we did not find, but one day's experience is worth a note.

We rode on from ten o'clock till three, without seeing a house, except a deserted cabin, or meeting a human being. We then came upon a ferry across a small stream or "bayou," near which was a collection of cabins. We asked the old negro who tended the ferry if we could get something to eat anywhere in the neighbourhood. He replied that his master sometimes took in travellers, and we had better call and try if the mistress wouldn't let us have some dinner.

The house was a small square log cabin, with a broad open shed or piazza in front, and a chimney, made of sticks and mud, leaning against one end. A smaller detached cabin, twenty feet in the rear, was used for a kitchen. A cistern under a roof, and collecting water from three roofs, stood between. The water from the bayou was not fit to drink, nor is the water of the Red River, or of any springs in this region. The people depend entirely on cisterns for drinking water. It is very little white folks need, however—milk, whisky, and, with the better class, Bordeaux wine, being the more common beverages.

About the house was a large yard, in which were two or three China trees, and two fine Cherokee roses; half a dozen hounds; several negro babies; turkeys and chickens, and a pet sow, teaching a fine litter of pigs how to root and wallow. Three hundred yards from the house was a [cotton] gin-house and stable, and in the interval between were two rows of comfortable negro cabins. . . .

---

[1] At this point, the narrative transitions to Olmsted's second journey, so the "we" here refers to his brother, John Hull, and himself. The rest of this chapter serves as a prelude to their far more extensive travels in Texas.

Entering the house, we found it to contain but a single room, about twenty feet by sixteen. Of this space one quarter was occupied by a bed—a great four-poster, with the curtains open, made up in the French style, with a strong furniture-calico day-coverlid. A smaller camp bed stood beside it. These two articles of furniture nearly filled the house on one side the door. At the other end was great log fireplace, with a fine fire. The outer door was left constantly open to admit the light. On one side the fire, next the door, was a table; a kind of dresser, with crockery, and a bureau stood on the other side, and there were two deer-skin seated chairs and one (Connecticut made) rocking chair.

A bold-faced, but otherwise good-enough-looking woman of a youngish middle age, was ironing a shirt on the table. We stated our circumstances, and asked if we could get some dinner from her. She reckoned we could, she said, if we'd wait till she was done ironing. So we waited, taking seats by the fire, and examining the literature and knick-knacks on the mantel-piece. These consisted of three Natchitoches *Chronicles*, a Patent Office Agricultural Report, "Christie's Galvanic Almanac," a Bible, "The Pirate of the Gulf," a powder-horn, the sheath of a bowie-knife, a whip-lash, and a tobacco-pipe.

Three of the hounds, a negro child, and a white child, had followed us to the door of the cabin, three chickens had entered before us, a cat and kittens were asleep in the corner of the fire-place. . . .

At length the woman finished her ironing, and went to the kitchen, whence quickly returning, she placed upon the table a plate of cold, salt, fat pork; a cup of what to both eye and tongue seemed lard, but which she termed butter; a plate of very stale, dry, flaky . . . corn-bread; a jug of molasses, and a pitcher of milk.

"Well, now it's ready, if you'll eat it," she said, turning to us. "Best we've got. Sit up. Take some pone"; and she sat down in the rocker at one end of the table. We took seats at the other end.

"Jupiter! what's the matter with this child?" A little white child that had crawled up into the gallery, and now to my side—flushed face, and wheezing like a high-pressure steamboat.

"Got the croup, I reckon," answered the woman. "Take some 'lasses."

The child crawled into the room. With the aid of a hand it stood up and walked round to its mother.

"How long has it been going on that way?" asked we.

"Well, it's been going on some days, now, and keeps getting worse. 'Twas right bad last night, in the night. Reckoned I should lose it, one spell. Take some butter."

We were quite faint with hunger when we rode up, but didn't eat much of the corn-cake and pork. The woman and the high-pressure child sat still and watched us, and we sat still and did our best, making much of the milk.

"Have you had a physician to see that child?" asked my brother, drawing back his chair.

She had not.

"Will you come to me, my dear?"

The child came to him, he felt its pulse and patted its hot forehead, looked down its throat, and leaned his ear on its chest.

"Are you a doctor, sir?"

"Yes, madam."

"Got some fever, hasn't it?"

"Yes."

"Not nigh so much as't had last night."

"Have you done anything for it?"

"Well, thar was a gentleman here; he told me sweet ile [corn] and sugar would be good for't, and I gave it a good deal of that: made it sick, it did. I thought, perhaps, that would do it good."

"Yes. You have had something like this in your family before, haven't you? You don't seem much alarmed."

"Oh yes, sir; that ar one" (pointing to [a] frowzy girl, whose name was Angelina) "had it two or three times — onst most as bad as this. All my children have had it. Is she bad, doctor?"

"Yes. I should say this was a very serious thing."

"Have you any medicine in the house?" he asked, after the woman had returned from a journey to the kitchen. She opened a drawer of the bureau, half full of patent medicines and some common drugs. "There's a whole heap o' truck in thar. I don't know what it all is. Whatever you want just help yourself. I can't read writin'; you must pick it out."

Such as were available were taken out and given to the mother, with directions about administering them, which she promised to obey. "But the first and most important thing for you to do is to shut the door, and make up the fire, and put the child to bed, and try to keep this wind off her."

"Lord! sir, you can't keep *her* in bed — she's too wild."

"Well, you must put some more clothes on her. Wrap her up, and try to keep her warm. The very best thing you can do for her is to give her a warm bath. Have you not got a washing tub?"

"Oh! yes, sir, I can do that. She'll go to bed pretty early; she's used to going 'tween sundown and dark."

"Well, give her the warm bath, then, and if she gets worse send for a physician immediately. You must be very careful of her, madam."

We walked to the stable, and as the horses had not finished eating their corn, I lounged about the quarters, and talked with the negro.

There was not a single soul in the quarters or in sight of the house except ourselves, the woman and her children, and the old negro. The negro women must have taken their sucklings with them, if they had any, to the field where they were at work.

The old man said they had "ten or eleven field-hands, such as they was," and his master would sell sixty to seventy bags of cotton: besides which they made all the corn and pork they wanted, and something over, and raised some cattle. . . .

When our horses were ready, we paid the negro for taking care of them, and I went in and asked the woman what I might pay her.

"What!" she asked, looking in my face as if angry.

I feared she was offended by my offering money for her hospitality, and put the question again as delicately as I could. She continued her sullen gaze at me for a moment, and then answered as if the words had been bullied out of her by a Tombs lawyer—[2]

"Dollar, I reckon."

"What!" thought I, but handed her the silver.

Riding out at the bars let down for us by the old negro, we wondered if the child would be living twenty-four hours later, and if it survived, what its moral chances were. Poor, we thought. Five miles from a neighbour; ten, probably, from a Louisiana school; hound-pups and negroes for playmates.

[2] "Tombs lawyer" is a term for a lawyer who hovered around a precinct court in mid-nineteenth-century New York City to fleece unsuspecting clients by agreeing to take their cases and then abandoning them once paid.

41. "THE MOST PROFITABLE ESTATE THAT I VISITED"

I have [previously] described in detail . . . two large plantations, which were much the best in respect to the happiness of the negroes, of all that I saw in the South.[1] I am now about to describe what I judged to be the most profitable estate that I visited. . . . It was situated upon a tributary

[1] The Georgia rice plantation of Mr. X. and the Louisiana sugar plantation of Mr. R.; see Selections 16 and 33. "The most profitable estate" that Olmsted is about to describe consisted of plantations that the editors of *The Papers of Frederick Law Olmsted*, based on

of the Mississippi [near Colfax, Louisiana], and accessible only by occasional steamboats; even this mode of communication being frequently interrupted at low stages of the rivers. The slaves upon it formed about one twentieth of the whole population of the county, in which the blacks considerably outnumber the whites. At the time of my visit, the owner was sojourning upon it, with his family and several invited guests, but his usual residence was upon a small plantation, of little productive value, situated in a neighbourhood somewhat noted for the luxury and hospitality of its citizens, and having a daily mail, and direct railroad and telegraphic communication with New York. This was, if I am not mistaken, his second visit in five years.

The property consisted of four adjoining plantations, each with its own negro-cabins, stables, and overseer, and each worked to a great extent independently of the others, but all contributing their crop to one [cotton-]gin-house and warehouse, and all under the general superintendence of a bailiff or manager, who constantly resided upon the estate, and in the absence of the owner, had vice-regal power over the overseers, controlling, so far as he thought fit, the economy of all the plantations.

The manager was himself a gentleman of good education, generous and poetic in temperament, and possessing a capacity for the enjoyment of nature and a happiness in the bucolic life, unfortunately rare with Americans. I found him a delightful companion, and I have known no man with whose natural tastes and feelings I have felt, on so short acquaintance, a more hearty sympathy.

The gang of toiling negroes to him, however, was as essential an element of the poetry of nature as flocks of peaceful sheep and herds of lowing [cows] . . . The overseers were superior to most of their class, and, with one exception, frank, honest, temperate, and industrious, but their feelings toward negroes were such as naturally result from their occupation. They were all married, and lived with their families, each in a cabin or cottage, in the hamlet of the slaves of which he had especial charge. Their wages varied from $500 to $1,000 a year each.

---

circumstantial evidence, have concluded were owned by a man named Meredith Calhoun of Colfax, Louisiana.

42. LIFE IN THE SLAVE QUARTERS

In the main, the negroes appeared to be well taken care of and abundantly supplied with the necessaries of vigorous physical existence. A large part of them lived in commodious and well-built cottages, with broad galleries in front, so that each family of five had two rooms on the lower floor, and a loft. The remainder lived in log huts, small and mean in appearance, but those of their overseers were little better, and preparations were being made to replace of these by neat boarded cottages. Each family had a fowl-house and hog-sty (constructed by the negroes themselves), and kept fowls and swine, feeding the latter during the summer on weeds and fattening them in the autumn on corn, *stolen* (this was mentioned to me by the overseers as if it were a matter of course) from their master's corn-fields.

I several times saw gangs of them eating the dinner which they had brought, each man for himself, to the field, and observed that they generally had plenty, often more than they could eat, of bacon, corn-bread, and molasses. The allowance food is weighed and measured under the eye of the manager by the drivers, and distributed to the head of each family weekly: consisting of—for each person, 3 pounds of pork, 1 peck of meal; and from January to July, 1 quart of molasses. Monthly, in addition, 1 pound tobacco, and 4 pints salt. No drink is ever served but water, except after unusual exposure, or to ditchers working in water, who get a glass of whisky at night. All hands cook for themselves after work at night, or whenever they please between nightfall and daybreak, each family in its own cabin. Each family has a garden, the products of which, together with eggs, fowls and bacon, they frequently sell, or use in addition to their regular allowance of food. Most of the families buy a barrel of flour every year. The manager endeavours to encourage this practice; and that they may spend their money for flour instead of liquor, he furnishes it to them at rather less than what it costs him at whole sale. There are many poor whites within a few miles who will always sell liquor to the negroes, and encourage them to steal, to obtain the means to buy it of them. These poor whites are always spoken of with anger by the overseers, and they each have a standing offer of much more than the intrinsic value of their land, from the manager, to induce them to move away.

The negroes also obtain a good deal of game. They set traps for raccoons, rabbits, and turkeys; and I once heard the stock-tender complaining that he had detected one of the vagabond whites stealing a turkey which had been caught in his pen. I several times partook of game, while on the plantation, that had been purchased of the negroes. . . .

The first morning I was on the estate, while at breakfast with the manager, an old negro woman came into the room and said to him, "Dat gal's bin bleedin' agin dis mornin'."

"How much did she bleed?"

"About a pint, sir."

"Very well: I'll call and see her after breakfast."

"I come up for some sugar of lead, masser; I gin her some powdered alum 'fore I come away."

"Very well; you can have some."

After breakfast the manager invited me to ride with him on his usual daily round of inspection through the plantations.

On reaching the nearest "quarters," we stopped at a house, a little larger than the ordinary cabins, which was called the loom-house, in which a dozen negroes were at work making shoes, and manufacturing coarse cotton stuff for negro clothing. One of the hands so employed was insane, and most of the others were cripples, invalids with chronic complaints, or unfitted by age, or some infirmity, for field-work.

From this we went to one of the cabins, where we found the sick woman who had been bleeding at the lungs, with the old nurse in attendance upon her. The manager examined and prescribed for her in a kind manner. When we came out he asked the nurse if any one else was sick.

"Oney dat woman Carline."

"What do you think is the matter with her?"

"Well, I don't tink dere's anyting de matter wid her, masser; I mus' answer you for true, I don't tink anyting de matter wid her, oney she's a little sore from dat whippin' she got."

We went to another cabin and entered a room where a woman lay on a bed, groaning. It was a dingy, comfortless room, but a musquito bar [mosquito net], much patched and very dirty, covered the bed. The manager asked the woman several times what was the matter, but could get no distinct reply. She appeared to be suffering great pain. The manager felt her pulse and looked at her tongue, and after making a few more inquiries, to which no intelligible reply was given, told her he did not believe she was ill at all. At this the woman's groans redoubled. "I have heard of your tricks," continued the manager; "you had a chill when I came to see you yesterday morning; you had a chill when the mistress came here, and you had a chill when the master came. I never knew a chill to last the whole day. So you'll just get up now and go to the field, and if you don't work smart, you'll get a dressing; do you hear?"

We then left. The manager said that he rarely—almost never—had occasion to employ a physician for the people. Never for accouchements [such as childbirth]; the women, from their labour in the field, were not subject to the difficulty, danger, and pain which attended women of the better classes in giving birth to their offspring. (I do not suppose that there was a physician within a day's journey of the plantations.)

Near the first quarters we visited there was a large blacksmith's and wheelwright's shop, in which a number of mechanics were at work. Most of them, as we rode up, were eating their breakfast, which they warmed at their fires. Within and around the shop there were some fifty ploughs which they were putting in order. The manager inspected the work, found some of it faulty, sharply reprimanded the workmen for not getting on faster, and threatened one of them with a whipping for not paying closer attention to the directions which had been given him.

The overseer of this plantation rode up while we were at the shop, and in a free and easy style, reported to the manager how all his hands were employed. There were so many at this and so many at that, and they had done so much since yesterday. "There's that girl, Caroline," said the manager; "she's not sick, and I told her she must go to work; put her to the hoeing; there's nothing the matter with her, except she's sore with the whipping she got. You must go and get her out." A woman passing at the time, the manager told her to go and tell Caroline she must get up and go to work, or the overseer would come and start her. She returned in a few minutes, and reported that Caroline said she could not get up. The overseer and manager rode toward the cabin, but before they reached it, the girl, who had probably been watching us from the window, came out and went to the field with her hoe. They then returned to me and continued their conversation.

Just before we left the overseer, he said, "I think that girl who ran away last week was in her cabin last night." The manager told me, as we rode on, that the people often ran away after they had been whipped, or something else had happened to make them angry. They hide in the swamp, and come in to the cabins at night to get food. They seldom remain away more than a fortnight, and when they come in they are whipped. The woman, Caroline, he said, had been delivered of a dead child about six weeks before, and had been complaining and getting rid of work ever since. She was the laziest woman on the estate. This shamming illness gave him the most disagreeable duty he had to perform.

Negroes were famous for it. "If it was not for her bad character," he continued, "I should fear to make her go to work to-day; but her pulse is steady, and her tongue perfectly smooth. We have to be sharp with them; if we were not, every negro on the estate would be a-bed."

We rode on to where the different gangs of labourers were at work and inspected them one after another. I observed, as we were looking at one of the gangs, that they were very dirty. "Negroes are the filthiest people in the world," said the manager; "there are some of them who would not keep clean twenty-four hours at a time if you gave them thirty suits a year." I asked him if there were any rules to maintain cleanliness. There were not, but sometimes the negroes were told at night that any one who came into the field the next morning without being clean would be whipped. This gave no trouble to those who were habitually clean, while it was in itself a punishment to those who were not, as they were obliged to spend the night in washing.

They were furnished with two suits of summer, and one of winter clothing each year. Besides which, most of them got presents of holi-day finery (calico dresses, handkerchiefs, etc.), and purchased more for themselves, at Christmas. One of the drivers now in the field had on a uniform coat of an officer of artillery. After the Mexican war, a great deal of military clothing was sold at auction in New Orleans, and much of it was bought by the planters at a low price, and given to their negroes, who were greatly pleased with it.

43. OVERSEERS AND DRIVERS

Each overseer regulated the hours of work on his own plantation. I saw the negroes at work before sunrise and after sunset. At about eight o'clock they were allowed to stop for breakfast, and again about noon, to dine. The length of these rests was at the discretion of the overseer or drivers, usually, I should say, from half an hour to an hour. There was no rule.

The number of hands directed by each overseer was considerably over one hundred. The manager thought it would be better economy to have a white man over every fifty hands, but the difficulty of obtaining trustworthy overseers prevented it. Three of those he then had were the best he had ever known. He described the great majority as being passionate, careless, inefficient men, generally intemperate, and totally unfitted for the duties of the position. The best overseers, ordinarily, are young men, the sons of small planters, who take up the business

temporarily, as a means of acquiring a little capital with which to purchase negroes for themselves.

The ploughs at work, both with single and double mule teams, were
generally held by women, and very well held, too. I watched with some
interest for any indication that their sex unfitted them for the occupation. Twenty of them were ploughing together, with double teams and
heavy ploughs. They were superintended by a negro man who carried
a whip, which he frequently cracked at them, permitting no dawdling
or delay at the turning; and they twitched their ploughs around on the
head-land, jerking their reins, and yelling to their mules, with apparent
ease, energy, and rapidity.

Throughout the South-west the negroes, as a rule, appear to be
worked much harder than in the Eastern and Northern Slave States.
I do not think they accomplish as much in the same time as agricultural labourers at the North usually do, but they certainly labour much
harder, and more unremittingly. They are constantly and steadily driven
up to their work, and the stupid, plodding, machine-like manner in which
they labour, is painful to witness. This was especially the case with the
hoe-gangs. One of them numbered nearly two hundred hands (for the
force of two plantations was working together), moving across the field
in parallel lines, with a considerable degree of precision. I repeatedly
rode through the lines at a canter, with other horsemen, often coming
upon them suddenly, without producing the smallest change or interruption in the dogged action of the labourers, or causing one of them, so
far as I could see, to lift an eye from the ground. I had noticed the same
thing with smaller numbers before, but here, considering that I was a
stranger, and that strangers could but very rarely visit the plantation,
it amazed me very much. I think it told a more painful story than any I
had ever heard, of the cruelty of slavery. It was emphasized by a tall and
powerful negro who walked to and fro in the rear of the line, frequently
cracking his whip, and calling out in the surliest manner, to one and
another, "Shove your hoe, there! shove your hoe!" But I never saw him
strike any one with the whip.

The whip was evidently in constant use, however. There were no
rules on the subject, that I learned; the overseers and drivers punished
the negroes whenever they deemed it necessary, and in such manner,
and with such severity, as they thought fit. "If you don't work faster,"
or "If you don't work better," or "If you don't recollect what I tell you, I
will have you flogged," I often heard. I said to one of the overseers, "It
must be disagreeable to have to punish them as much as you do." "Yes,
it would be to those who are not used to it—but it's my business, and I

careful

think nothing of it. Why, sir, I wouldn't mind killing a nigger more than I would a dog." I asked if he had ever killed a negro. "Not quite that," he said, but overseers were often obliged to.

44. THE RELIGIOUS INSTRUCTION OF SLAVES

Being with the proprietor and the manager together, I asked about the religious condition of the slaves. There were "preachers" on the plantations, and they had some religious observances on a Sunday; but the preachers were the worst characters among them, and, they thought, only made their religion a cloak for habits of especial depravity. They were, at all events, the most deceitful and dishonest slaves on the plantation, and oftenest required punishment. The negroes of all denominations, and even those who ordinarily made no religious pretensions, would join together in exciting religious observances. They did not like to have white men preach on the estate; and in future they did not intend to permit them to do so. It excited the negroes so much as to greatly interfere with the subordination and order which were necessary to obtain the profitable use of their labour. They would be singing and dancing every night in their cabins, till dawn of day, and utterly unfit themselves for work.

With regard to the religious instruction of slaves, widely different practices of course prevail. There are some slaveholders, like Bishop [Leonidas] Polk of Louisiana,[1] who oblige, and many others who encourage, their slaves to engage in religious exercises, furnishing them certain conveniences for the purpose. Among the wealthier slaveowners, however, and in all those parts of the country where the enslaved portion of the population outnumbers the whites, there is generally a visible, and often an avowed distrust of the effect of religious exercises upon slaves, and even the preaching of white clergymen to them is permitted by many with reluctance. The prevailing impression among us, with regard to the important influence of slavery in promoting the spread of religion among the blacks, is an erroneous one in my opinion. I have heard Northern clergymen speak as if they supposed a regular

[1] Leonidas Polk was a prominent bishop who headed the Epicospal Diocese of Louisiana for much of the 1840s and 1850s and was himself a large slaveholder. A Confederate general during the Civil War, he became known as "the Fighting Bishop." He was actually a fellow guest during Olmsted's visit to these plantations. Olmsted wrote of him: "He assured me that he had been all over the country on the Red River, the scene of the fictitious sufferings of 'Uncle Tom,' and that he had found the temporal and spiritual welfare of the negroes well cared for."

daily instruction of slaves in the truths of Christianity to be general. So far is this from being the case that, although family prayers were held in several of the fifty planters' houses in Mississippi and Alabama, in which I passed a night, I never in a single instance saw a field-hand attend or join the devotion of the family.

45. THE ECONOMY OF COTTON

It may be computed, from the census of 1850, that about one half the slaves of Louisiana and one third those of Mississippi, belonged to estates of not less than fifty slaves each, and of these, I believe, nine-tenths live on plantations which their owners reside upon, if at all, but transiently.

The number of plantations of this class, and the proportion of those employed upon them to the whole body of negroes in the country, is, as I have said, rapidly increasing. At the present prices of cotton the large grower has such advantages over the small, that the owner of a plantation of fifty slaves, favourably situated, unless he lives very recklessly, will increase in wealth so rapidly and possess such a credit that he may very soon establish or purchase other plantations, so that at his death his children may be provided for without reducing the effective force of negroes on any division of his landed estate. The excessive credit given to such planters by negro dealers and tradesmen renders this the more practicable. The higher the price of cotton the higher is that of negroes, and the higher the price of negroes the less is it in the power of men of small capital to buy them. Large plantations of course pay a much larger per centage on the capital invested in them than smaller ones; indeed the only plausible economical defence of slavery is simply an explanation of the advantages of associated labour, advantages which are possessed equally by large manufacturing establishments in which free labourers are brought together and employed in the most effective manner, and which I can see no sufficient reason for supposing could not be made available for agriculture did not the good results flowing from small holdings, on the whole, counterbalance them. If the present high price of cotton and the present scarcity of labour at the South continue, the cultivation of cotton on small plantations will by-and-by become unusual, for the same reason that hand-loom weaving has become unusual in the farm houses of Massachusetts.

But whatever advantages large plantations have, they accrue only to their owners and to the buyers of cotton; the mass of the white inhabitants are dispersed over a greater surface, discouraged and driven toward barbarism by them, and the blacks upon them, while rapidly degenerating from all that is redeeming in savage-life, are, it is to be feared, gaining little that is valuable of civilization.

In the report of the Grand Jury of Richland District, South Carolina, in 1854, calling for a re-establishment of the African slave trade, it is observed: "As to the morality of this question, it is scarcely necessary for us to allude to it; when the fact is remarked that the plantations of Alabama, Mississippi, Louisiana, and Texas have been and are daily settled by the removal of slaves from the more northern of the Slave States, and that in consequence of their having been raised in a more healthy climate and in most cases trained to pursuits totally different, the mortality even on the best-ordered farms is so great that in many instances the entire income is expended in the purchase of more slaves from the same source in order to replenish and keep up those plantations, while in *every case* the condition of the slave, if his life is spared, is made worse both physically and morally. . . ."

I believe that this statement gives an exaggerated and calumnious [slanderous] report of the general condition of the slaves upon the plantations of the States referred to—containing, as they do, nearly one half of the whole slave population of the South—but I have not been able to resist the conviction that in the districts where cotton is now grown most profitably to the planters, the oppression and deterioration of the negro race is much more lamentable than is generally supposed by those who like myself have been constrained, by other considerations, to accept it as a duty to oppose temperately but determinately the modern policy of the South, of which this is an immediate result. Its effect on the white race, I still consider to be infinitely more deplorable.

Chapter 4

On to Texas and Back to Louisiana

Certainly the most substantive deletion Olmsted and his editing partner, Daniel Goodloe, made in condensing his earlier writings involved his journey to Texas. Less than 80 of the original 516 pages of A Journey through Texas *appear in* The Cotton Kingdom. *Olmsted's rationale seems to have been the disproportionate attention given to a single state (though it was a state in which he and his brother spent nearly five months, from December 20, 1853, to May 17, 1854, far more time than he spent in any other southern state). It may also have been that when they were compiling* The Cotton Kingdom *during the first weeks of the Civil War, Texas seemed less relevant than did other Confederate states, particularly central and west Texas, sections beyond the cotton belt and heavy slaveholding areas of east Texas. Thus, in keeping with the central themes of this 1861 volume, it was those issues as observed and experienced in east Texas that appear in* The Cotton Kingdom *and are included here.*

Olmsted was struck throughout his travels by how many southerners and other Americans were interested in Texas and how many he encountered who were actually moving west to settle there. The first selection here picks up where the last chapter left off—in Natchitoches, Louisiana, where Olmsted most fully confronted that wave of migration, a wave he and his brother briefly joined as they prepared for their adventure in the Lone Star State (see map, page 11). A few selections then discuss the Olmsteds' experiences in Texas, including a brief incident involving a runaway slave caught in Houston (Selection 49), after which the chapter shifts to Opelousas, in south-central Louisiana, the heart of Creole country, on which Olmsted offers extended insights. Shortly thereafter, he and his brother went their separate ways, which marked the divide between Olmsted's second and third journeys, and between this chapter and the next.

46. ON THE EMIGRANT ROAD INTO TEXAS

Five minutes' ride took us deep into the pines. Natchitoches, and with it all the tumult and bother of social civilization, had disappeared. Under the pines and beyond them was a new, calm, free life, upon which we entered with a glow of enthusiasm, which, however, hardly sufficed to light up a whole day of pine shadows, and many times afterwards glimmered very dull over days on days of cold corn-bread and cheerless winter prairies.

For two days, we rode through these pines over a sandy surface, having little rise and fall, watered here and there by small creeks and ponds, within reach of whose overflow, present or past, stand deciduous trees, such as, principally, oaks and cotton-woods, in a firmer and richer soil. Wherever the road crosses or approaches these spots, there is or has been, usually, a plantation.

The road could hardly be called a road. It was only a way where people had passed along before. Each man had taken such a path as suited him, turning aside to avoid, on high ground, the sand; on low ground, the mud. We chose, generally, the untrodden elastic pavement of pine leaves, at a little distance from the main track.

We overtook, several times in the course of each day, the slow emigrant trains, for which this road, though less frequented than years ago, is still a chief thoroughfare. Inexorable destiny it seems that drags or drives on, always Westward, these toilworn people. Several families were frequently moving together, coming from the same district, or chance met and joined, for company, on the long road from Alabama, Georgia, or the Carolinas. Before you come upon them you hear, ringing through the woods, the fierce cries and blows with which they urge on their jaded cattle. Then the stragglers appear, lean dogs or fainting negroes, ragged and spiritless. An old granny, hauling on, by the hand, a weak boy—too old to ride and too young to keep up. An old man, heavily loaded, with a rifle. Then the white covers of the waggons, jerking up and down as they mount over a root or plunge into a rut, disappearing, one after another, where the road descends. . . .

We passed in the day perhaps one hundred persons attached to these trains, probably an unusual number; but the immigration this year had been retarded and condensed by the fear of yellow fever, the last case of which, at Natchitoches, had indeed begun only the night before our arrival. Our chances of danger were considered small, however, as the hard frosts had already come. One of these trains was made up of three large waggons, loaded with furniture, babies, and invalids, two or three light waggons, and a gang of twenty able field-hands. They travel ten or fifteen miles a day, stopping wherever night over-takes them. The masters are plainly dressed, often in home-spun, keeping their eyes about them, noticing the soil, sometimes making a remark on the crops by the roadside; but generally dogged, surly, and silent. The women are silent too, frequently walking, to relieve the teams; and weary, haggard, mud be-draggled, forlorn, and disconsolate, yet hopeful and careful. The negroes, mud-incrusted, wrapped in old blankets or gunny-bags, suffering from cold, plod on, aimless, hopeless, thoughtless, more indifferent, apparently, than the oxen, to all about them. . . .

The [Louisiana] country was very similar to that passed over the day before, with perhaps rather more of the cultivable loam. A good part of the land had, at some time, been cleared, but much was already turned over to the "old-field pines," some of them even fifteen years or more. In fact, a larger area had been abandoned, we thought, than remained under cultivation. With the land, many cabins have, of course, also been deserted, giving the road a desolate air. If you ask, where are the people that once occupied these, the universal reply is, "Gone to Texas."

The plantations occur, perhaps, at an average distance of three or four miles. Most of the remaining inhabitants live chiefly, to appearances, by fleecing emigrants. Every shanty sells spirits, and takes in travellers. We passed through but one village, which consisted of six dwellings. The families obtained their livelihood by the following occupations: one by shoeing the horses of emigrants; one by repairing the wheels of their waggons; one by selling them groceries. The smallest cabin contained a physician. It was not larger than a good-sized medicine chest, but had the biggest sign. The others advertised "corn and fodder." The prices charged for any article sold, or service performed, were enormous; full one hundred per cent. over those of New Orleans.

We met Spaniards once or twice on the road, and the population of this district is thought to be one half of Spanish origin. They have no houses on the road, however, but live in little hamlets in the forest, or in cabins contiguous to each other, about a pond. They make no progress in acquiring capital of their own, but engage in hunting and fishing, or in herding cattle for larger proprietors of the land. For this business they seem to have an hereditary adaptation, far excelling negroes of equal experience.

47. HOTEL CONVERSATION WITH SIX TEXANS

[*East Texas*]. — Late in the same evening we reached a hamlet [Caldwell, about ninety miles east of Austin], the "seat of justice" of Burleson County. . . .

The "hotel" was an unusually large and fine one; the principal room had glass windows. Several panes of these were, however, broken, and the outside door could not be closed from without; and when closed, was generally pried open with a pocket-knife by those who wished to go out. A great part of the time it was left open. Supper was served in another room, in which there was no fire, and the outside door was left open for the convenience of the servants in passing to and from the kitchen, which, as usual here at large houses, was in a detached building. Supper was, however, eaten with such rapidity that nothing had time to freeze on the table.

There were six Texans, planters and herdsmen, who had made harbour at the inn for the norther [cold gale from the north], two German shopkeepers and a young lawyer, who were boarders, besides our party of three,[1] who had to be seated before the fire. We kept coats and hats on, and gained as much warmth, from the friendly manner in which we drew together, as possible. After ascertaining, by a not at all impertinent or inconsiderate method of inquiry, where we were from, which way we were going, what we thought of the country, what we thought of the weather, and what were the capacities and the cost of our fire-arms, we were considered as initiated members of the crowd, and "the conversation became general."

The matter of most interest came up in this wise: "The man made a white boy, fourteen or fifteen years old, get up and go out in the norther for wood, when there was a great, strong nigger fellow lying on the floor doing nothing. God! I had an appetite to give him a hundred [lashes], right there."

"Why, you wouldn't go out into the norther yourself, would you, if you were not obliged to?" inquired one, laughingly.

"I wouldn't have a nigger in my house that I was afraid to set to work, at anything I wanted him to do, at any time. They'd hired him out to go to a new place next Thursday, and they were afraid if they didn't treat him well, he'd run away. If I couldn't break a nigger of running away, I wouldn't have him any how."

"I can tell you how you can break a nigger of running away, certain," said another. "There was an old fellow I used to know in Georgia, that always cured his so. If a nigger ran away, when he caught him, he would bind his knee over a log, and fasten him so he couldn't stir; then he'd take a pair of pincers and pull one of his toe-nails out by the roots; and tell him that if he ever run away again, he would pull out two of them, and if he run away again after that, he told them he'd pull out four of them, and so on, doubling each time. He never had to do it more than twice—it always cured them."

One of the company then said that he was at the present time in pursuit of a negro. He had bought him of a relative in Mississippi, and had been told that he was a great runaway. He had, in fact, run away from his relative three times, and always when they caught him he was trying to *get back to Illinois*;[2] that was the reason he sold him. "He offered him to me cheap," he continued, "and I bought him because he was a first-rate nigger, and I thought perhaps I could break him of running away by bringing him down to this new country. I expect he's making

<hr>

[1] The Olmsted brothers' "party of three" included a guide, identified only as Mr. B.
[2] [Olmsted] Many freemen have been kidnapped in Illinois and sold into slavery.

for Mexico now. I am a-most sure I saw his tracks on the road about twelve miles back, where he was a-coming on this way. Night before last I engaged with a man who's got some first-rate nigger dogs to meet me here to-night; but I suppose the cold keeps him back." He then asked us to look out for him as we went on west, and gave us a minute description of him that we might recognize him. He was "a real black nigger," and carried off a double-barrelled gun with him. Another man, who was going on by another road westward, offered to look for him that way, and to advertise him. Would he be likely to defend himself with the gun if he should try to secure him? he asked. The owner said he had no doubt he would. He was as humble a nigger when he was at work as ever he had seen; but he was a mighty resolute nigger—there was no man had more resolution. "Couldn't I induce him to let me take the gun by pretending I wanted to look at it, or something? I'd talk to him simple; make as if I was a stranger, and ask him about the road, and so on, and finally ask him what he had got for a gun, and to let me look at it." The owner didn't believe he'd let go of the gun; he was a "nigger of sense—as much sense as a white man; he was not one of your kinkey-headed niggers." The chances of catching him were discussed. Some thought they were good, and some that the owner might almost as well give it up, he'd got such a start. It was three hundred miles to the Mexican frontier, and he'd have to make fires to cook the game he would kill, and could travel only at night; but then every nigger or Mexican he could find would help him, and if he had so much sense, he'd manage to find out his way pretty straight, and yet not have white folks see him.

48. A NORTHERN TRANSPLANT AND HER SLAVES

Remarking, one day, at the house of a woman who was brought up at the North, that there was much more comfort at her house than any we had previously stopped at, she told us that the only reason the people didn't have any comfort here was, that they wouldn't *take any trouble* to get anything. Anything that their negroes could make they would eat; but they would take no pains to instruct them, or to get anything that didn't grow on the plantation. A neighbour of hers owned fifty cows, she supposed, but very rarely had any milk and scarcely ever any butter, simply because his people were too lazy to milk or churn, and he wouldn't take the trouble to make them.

This woman entirely sustained the assertion that Northern people, when they come to the South, have less feeling for the negroes than Southerners themselves usually have. We asked her (she lived in a village) whether she hired or owned her servants. They owned them all, she said. When they first came to Texas they hired servants, but it was very troublesome; they would take no interest in anything; and she couldn't get along with them. Then very often their owners, on some pretext (ill-treatment, perhaps), would take them away. Then they bought negroes. It was very expensive: a good negro girl cost seven or eight hundred dollars, and that, we must know, was a great deal of money to be laid out in a thing that might lie right down the next day and die. They were not much better either than the hired servants.

Folks up North talked about how badly the negroes were treated; she wished they could see how much work her girls did. She had four of them, and she knew they didn't do half so much work as one good Dutch girl such as she used to have at the North. Oh! the negroes were the laziest things in creation; there was no knowing how much trouble they gave to look after them. Up to the North, if a girl went out into the garden for anything, when she came back she would clean her feet, but these nigger girls will stump right in and track mud all over the house. What do they care? They'd just as lief [soon] clean the mud after themselves as anything else—their time isn't any value to themselves. What do they care for the trouble it gives you? Not a bit. And you may scold 'em and whip 'em—you never can break 'em into better habits.

I asked what were servants' wages when they were hired out to do housework? They were paid seven or eight dollars a month; sometimes ten. She didn't used to pay her girl at the North but four dollars, and she knew she would do more work than any six of the niggers, and not give half so much trouble as one. But you couldn't get any other help here but niggers. Northern folks talk about abolishing slavery, but there wouldn't be any use in that; that would be ridiculous, unless you could some way get rid of the niggers. Why, they'd murder us all in our beds—that's what they'd do. Why, over to Fannin, there was a negro woman that killed her mistress with an axe, and her two little ones. The people just flocked together, and hung her right up on the spot; they ought to have piled some wood round her, and burned her to death; that would have been a good lesson to the rest. We afterwards heard [our hostess] scolding one of her girls, the girl made some exculpatory [defensive] reply, and getting the best of the argument, the mistress angrily told her if she said another word she would have two hundred lashes given her. She came in and remarked that if she hadn't felt so nervous she would have given that girl a good whipping herself; these niggers are so saucy, it's very trying to one who has to take care of them.

Servants are, it is true, "a trial," in all lands, ages, and nations. But note the fatal reason this woman frankly gives for the inevitable delinquencies of slave-servants, "Their time isn't any value to themselves!"

The women of Eastern Texas seemed to us, in general, far superior to their lords. They have, at least, the tender hearts and some of the gentle delicacy that your "true Texan" lacks, whether mistresses of slaves, or only of their own frying-pan. They are over-worked, however, as soon as married, and care gives them thin faces, sallow complexions, and expressions either sad or sour.

49. A RUNAWAY CAUGHT IN HOUSTON

Houston. —We were sitting on the gallery of the hotel. A tall, jet black negro came up, leading by a rope a downcast mulatto, whose hands were lashed by a cord to his waist, and whose face was horribly cut, and dripping with blood. The wounded man crouched and leaned for support against one of the columns of the gallery—faint and sick.

"What's the matter with that boy?" asked a smoking lounger.

"I run a fork into his face," answered the negro.

"What are his hands tied for?"

"He's a runaway, sir."

"Did you catch him?"

"Yes, sir. He was hiding in the hay-loft, and when I went up to throw some hay to the horses, I pushed the fork down into the mow and it struck something hard. I didn't know what it was, and I pushed hard, and gave it a turn, and then he hollered, and I took it out."

"What do you bring him here for?"

"Come for the key of the jail, sir, to lock him up."

"What!" said another, "one darkey catch another darkey? Don't believe that story."

"Oh yes, mass'r, I tell for true. He was down in our hay-loft, and so you see when I stab him, I *have to* catch him."

"Why, he's hurt bad, isn't he?"

"Yes, he says I pushed through the bones."

"Whose nigger is he?"

"He says he belong to Mass'r Frost, sir, on the Brazos."

The key was soon brought, and the negro led the mulatto away to jail. He walked away limping, crouching, and writhing, as if he had received other injuries than those on his face. The bystanders remarked that the negro had not probably told the whole story.

We afterwards happened to see a gentleman on horseback, and smoking, leading by a long rope through the deep mud, out into the country, the poor mulatto, still limping and crouching, his hands manacled, and his arms pinioned.

There is a prominent slave-mart in town, which holds a large lot of likely-looking negroes, waiting purchasers. In the windows of shops, and on the doors and columns of the hotel, are many written advertisements, headed "A likely negro girl for sale." "Two negroes for sale." "Twenty negro boys for sale," etc.

50. CONVERSATION WITH A SLAVE TRADER IN OPELOUSAS

The distance to Opelousas [in Louisiana], [a] Frenchman told us, was fifteen miles by the road, though only ten miles in a direct line. We found it lined with farms, whose division-fences the road always followed, frequently changing its course in so doing at a right angle. The country was very wet and unattractive. About five miles from the town, begin plantations on an extensive scale, upon better soil, and here were large gangs of negroes at work upon cotton, with their hoes. . . .

On the gallery of the hotel, after dinner, a fine-looking man — who was on the best of terms with every one — familiar with the judge — and who had been particularly polite to me, at the dinner-table, said to another:

"I hear you were very unlucky with that girl you bought of me, last year."

"Yes, I was; very unlucky. She died with her first child, and the child died, too."

"Well, that was right hard for you. She was a fine girl. I don't reckon you lost less than five thousand dollars, when she died."

"No, sir, not a dollar less."

"Well, it came right hard upon you — just beginning so."

"Yes, I was foolish, I suppose, to risk so much on the life of a single woman; but I've got a good start again now, for all that. I've got two right likely girls; one of them's got a fine boy, four months old, and the other's with child — and old Pine Knot's as hearty as ever."

"Is he? Hasn't been sick at all, eh?"

"Yes; he was sick very soon after I bought him of you; but he got well soon."

"That's right. I'd rather a nigger would be sick early, after he comes into this country; for he's bound to be acclimated, sooner or later, and the longer it's put off, the harder it goes with, him."

The man was a regular negro trader. He told me that he had a partner in Kentucky, and that they owned a farm there, and another one here. His partner bought negroes, as opportunity offered to get them advantageously, and kept them on their Kentucky farm; and he went on occasionally, and brought the surplus to their Louisiana plantation—where he held them for sale.

"So-and-so is very hard upon you," said another man, to him as he still sat, smoking his cigar, on the gallery, after dinner.

"Why so? He's no business to complain; I told him just exactly what the nigger was, before I sold him" (laughing, as if there was a concealed joke). "It was all right—all right. I heard that he sold him again for a thousand dollars; and the people that bought him, gave him two hundred dollars to let them off from the bargain. I'm sure he can't complain of me. It was a fair transaction. He knew just what he was buying."

51. LOUISIANA CLASS DISTINCTIONS AND CREOLES

An intelligent man whom I met here, and who had been travelling most of the time during the last two years in Louisiana, having business with the planters, described the condition of the new slaveholders and the poorer planters as being very miserable.

He had sometimes found it difficult to get food, even when he was in urgent need of it, at their houses. The lowest class live much from hand to mouth, and are often in extreme destitution. This was more particularly the case with those who lived on the river; those who resided on the prairies were seldom so much reduced. The former now live only on those parts of the river to which the back-swamp approaches nearest; that is, where there is but little valuable land, that can be appropriated for plantation-purposes. They almost all reside in communities, very closely housed in poor cabins. If there is any considerable number of them, there is to be always found, among the cluster of their cabins, a church, and a billiard and a gambling-room—and the latter is always occupied, and play going on.

They almost all appear excessively apathetic, sleepy, and stupid, if you see them at home; and they are always longing and waiting for some excitement. They live for excitement, and will not labour, unless it is violently, for a short time, to gratify some passion.

This was as much the case with the women as the men. The women were often handsome, stately, and graceful, and, ordinarily, exceedingly kind; but languid, and incredibly indolent, unless there was a ball, or some other excitement, to engage them. Under excitement, they were splendidly animated, impetuous, and eccentric. One moment they seemed possessed by a devil, and the next by an angel.

The Creoles[1] are inveterate gamblers—rich and poor alike. The majority of wealthy Creoles, he said, do nothing to improve their estate; and are very apt to live beyond their income. They borrow and play, and keep borrowing to play, as long as they can; but they will not part with their land, and especially with their home, as long as they can help it, by any sacrifice.

The men are generally dissolute. They have large families, and a great deal of family affection. He did not know that they had more than Anglo-Saxons; but they certainly manifested a great deal more, and, he thought, had more domestic happiness. If a Creole farmer's child marries, he will build a house for the new couple, adjoining his own; and when another marries, he builds another house—so, often his whole front on the river is at length occupied. Then he begins to build others, back of the first—and so, there gradually forms a little village, wherever there is a large Creole family, owning any considerable piece of land. The children are poorly educated, and are not brought up to industry, at all.

The planters living near them, as their needs increase, lend them money, and get mortgages on their land, or, in some way or other, if it is of any value, force them to part with it. Thus they are every year reduced, more and more, to the poorest lands; and the majority now are able to get but a very poor living, and would not be able to live at all in a Northern climate. They are nevertheless—even the poorest of them—habitually gay and careless, as well as kind-hearted, hospitable, and dissolute—working little, and spending much of their time at church, or at balls, or the gaming-table.

There are very many wealthy Creole planters, who are as cultivated and intelligent as the better class of American planters, and usually more refined. The Creoles, he said, did not work their slaves as hard as

---

[1] [Olmsted] Creole means simply native of the region, but in Louisiana (a vast region purchased, by the United States, of France, for strategetic [sic] reasons, and now proposed to be filibustered away from us), it generally indicates French blood.

the Americans; but, on the other hand, they did not feed or clothe them nearly as well, and he had noticed universally, on the Creole plantations, a large number of "used-up hands"—slaves, sore and crippled, or invalided for some cause. On all sugar plantations, he said, they work the negroes excessively, in the grinding season; often cruelly. . . .

I remarked that the law, in Louisiana, required that meat should be regularly served to the negroes.

"O, those laws are very little regarded."

"Indeed?"

"Certainly. Suppose you are my neighbour; if you maltreat your negroes, and tell me of it, or I see it, am I going to prefer charges against you to the magistrates? I might possibly get you punished according to law; but if I did, or did not, I should have you, and your family and friends, far and near, for my mortal enemies. There is a law of the State that negroes shall not be worked on Sundays; but I have seen negroes at work almost every Sunday, when I have been in the country, since I have lived in Louisiana."[2]

[2] [Olmsted] I also saw slaves at work every Sunday that I was in Louisiana. The law permits slaves to be worked, I believe, on Sunday; but requires that some compensation shall be made to them when they are—such as a subsequent holiday.

52. CONTRASTING NEW YORK FARMERS AND LOUISIANA PLANTERS

He [the business traveler in conversation with Olmsted] had lived, when a boy, for several years on a farm in Western New York, and afterwards, for some time, at Rochester, and was well acquainted with the people generally, in the valley of the Genesee [River].

I asked him if he thought, among the intelligent class of farmers and planters, people of equal property lived more happily in New York or Louisiana. He replied immediately, as if he had carefully considered the topic, that, with some rare exceptions, farmers worth forty thousand dollars lived in far greater comfort, and enjoyed more refined and elegant leisure, than planters worth three hundred thousand, and that farmers of the ordinary class, who laboured with their own hands, and were worth some six thousand dollars, in the Genesee valley, lived in far greater comfort, and in all respects more enviably, than planters worth forty thousand dollars in Louisiana. The contrast was especially favourable to the New York farmer, in respect to books and newspapers. He might travel several days, and call on a hundred planters, and hardly see in their houses more than a single newspaper apiece, in most cases; perhaps none at all: nor any books, except a Bible, and some government publications, that had been franked [mailed at no cost] to them through the post-office, and perhaps a few religious tracts or school-books.

The most striking difference that he observed between the Anglo-Americans of Louisiana and New York, was the impulsive and unreflective habit of the former, in doing business. He mentioned, as illustrative of this, the almost universal passion among the planters for increasing their negro-stock. It appeared evident to him, that the market price of negroes was much higher than the prices of cotton and sugar warranted; but it seemed as if no planter ever made any calculation of that kind. The majority of planters, he thought, would always run in debt to the extent of their credit for negroes, whatever was asked for them, without making any calculation of the reasonable prospects of their being able to pay their debts. When any one made a good crop, he would always expect that his next one would be better, and make purchases in advance upon such expectation. When they were dunned, they would attribute their inability to pay, to accidental short crops, and always were going ahead risking everything, in confidence that another year of luck would favour them, and a big crop make all right.

If they had a full crop, probably there would be good crops everywhere else, and prices would fall, and then they would whine and complain, as if the merchants were to blame for it, and would insinuate that no one could be expected to pay his debts when prices were so low, and that it would be dangerous to press such an unjust claim. And, if the crops met with any misfortune, from floods, or rot, or vermin, they would cry about it like children when rain fell upon a holiday, as if they had never thought of the possibility of such a thing, and were very hard used.

Chapter 5

The "Back Country"

The final leg of Olmsted's southern journeys came after his brother left him and he continued for another two months of travel on his own. As John Hull returned to New Orleans and from there to New York by ship late in May 1854, Olmsted moved up the Mississippi River and then turned northeast, traveling through what he called the "interior cotton districts" of central Mississippi and northern Alabama before reaching

Chattanooga, Tennessee (see map, page 11). From there he proceeded through the Appalachian Mountains of western North Carolina, eastern Tennessee, and southwestern Virginia. His observations appeared first in print under the title A Journey in the Back Country, *the third volume of his travel chronicle, which was published in 1860, only a year before he incorporated much of it into* The Cotton Kingdom. *While the term "back country" is more applicable to the highland regions that made up the latter part of Olmsted's journey than to the central cotton belts of the Deep South, it is retained here to preserve Olmsted's own overarching label for the areas he covered during June and July 1854.*

The selections in this chapter reflect the mixed feelings about slavery expressed by various slaveholders and nonslaveholders whom Olmsted encountered along this route. The chapter begins with two episodes in central Mississippi that challenge our assumptions about Deep South planters being solidly in support of the institution. As Olmsted traveled in the Alabama hill country and then into the mountain South, he faced even more negative attitudes regarding slavery, with increasing hostility toward both the labor system and the planter class it spawned. None of this opposition arose from sympathy for the slaves themselves; the racism of these white southerners proved as rampant as that of any others.

The final entry provides one of the clearest examples of a major theme of Olmsted's—that owning slaves was no guarantee of a better life for southerners on the margins. Also apparent among southern highlanders were misconceptions and limited understanding of the rest of the South and the rest of the country, in particular Texas, which come through in exchanges that obviously interested, even dismayed, this now seasoned traveler.

53. DISCUSSIONS OF MEXICO AND RUNAWAY SLAVES

June 2nd. [Central Mississippi].—I met a ragged old negro, of whom I asked the way, and at what house within twelve miles I had better stop. He advised me to go to one more than twelve miles distant.

"I suppose," said I, "I can stop at any house along the road here, can't I? They'll all take in travellers?"

"Yes, sir, if you'll take rough fare, such as travellers has to, sometimes. They're all damn'd rascals along dis road, for ten or twelve miles, and you'll get nothin' but rough fare. But I say, massa, rough fare's good enough for dis world; ain't it, massa." . . .

. . .

A little after sunset I came to an unusually promising plantation, the dwelling being within a large enclosure, in which there was a well-kept southern sward [grassy area] shaded by fine trees. The house, of the usual form, was painted white, and the large number of neat outbuildings seemed to indicate opulence, and, I thought, unusual good taste in its owner. A lad of sixteen received me, and said I could stay; I might fasten my horse, and when the negroes came up he would have him taken care of. When I had done so, and had brought the saddle to the verandah, he offered me a chair, and at once commenced a conversation in the character of entertainer. Nothing in his tone or manner would have indicated that he was not the father of the family, and proprietor of the establishment. No prince royal could have had more assured and nonchalant dignity. Yet a Northern stable-boy, or apprentice, of his age, would seldom be found as ignorant.

"Where do you live, sir, when you are at home?" he asked.

"At New York."

"New York is a big place, sir, I expect?"

"Yes, very big."

"Big as New Orleans, is it, sir?"

"Yes, much bigger."

"Bigger'n New Orleans? It must be a bully city."

"Yes; the largest in America."

"Sickly there now, sir?"

"No, not now; it is sometimes."

"Like New Orleans, I suppose?"

"No, never so bad as New Orleans sometimes is."

"Right healthy place, I expect, sir?"

"Yes, I believe so, for a place of its size."

"What diseases do you have there, sir?"

"All sorts of diseases—not so much fever, however, as you have hereabouts."

"Measles and whooping-cough, sometimes, I reckon?"

"Yes, 'most all the time, I dare say."

"All the time! People must die there right smart. Some is dyin' 'most every day, I expect, sir?"

"More than a hundred every day, I suppose."

"Gosh! a hundred every day! Almighty sickly place 't must be?"

"It is such a large place, you see—seven hundred thousand people."

"Seven hundred thousand—expect that's a heap of people, ain't it?"

His father, a portly, well-dressed man, soon came in, and learning that I had been in Mexico,[1] said, "I suppose there's a heap of Americans flocking in and settling up that country along on the line, ain't there, sir?"

"No, sir, very few. I saw none, in fact—only a few Irishmen and Frenchmen, who called themselves Americans. Those were the only foreigners I saw, except negroes."

"Niggers! Where were they from?"

"They were runaways from Texas."

"But their masters go there and get them again, don't they?"

"No, sir, they can't."

"Why not?'

"The Mexicans are friendly to the niggers, and protect them."

"But why not go to the Government?"

"The Government considers them as free, and will not let them be taken back."

"But that's stealing, sir. Why don't our Government make them deliver them up? What good is the Government to us if it don't preserve the rights of property, sir? Niggers are property, ain't they? and if a man steals my property, ain't the Government bound to get it for me? Niggers are property, sir, the same as horses and cattle, and nobody's any more right to help a nigger that's run away than he has to steal a horse."

He spoke very angrily, and was excited. Perhaps he was indirectly addressing me, as a Northern man, on the general subject of fugitive slaves. I said that it was necessary to have special treaty stipulations about such matters. The Mexicans lost their *peóns*—bounden servants; they ran away to our side, but the United States Government never took any measures to restore them, nor did the Mexicans ask it. "But," he answered, in a tone of indignation, "those are not niggers, are they? They are white people, sir, just as white as the Mexicans themselves, and just as much right to be free."

---

[1] During their tour of Texas, the Olmsted brothers crossed the Mexican border, spending three days south of the Rio Grande in April 1854.

54. A SLAVEHOLDING ABOLITIONIST HOST

June 3rd. [*Madison County, Miss.*]—Yesterday I met a well-dressed man upon the road, and inquired of him if he could recommend me to a comfortable place to pass the night.

"Yes, I can," said he; "you stop at John Watson's. He is a real good fellow, and his wife is a nice, tidy woman; he's got a good house, and you'll be as well taken care of there as in any place I know."

"What I am most concerned about is a clean bed," said I.

"Well, you are safe for that, there."

So distinct a recommendation was unusual, and when I reached the house he had described to me, though it was not yet dark, I stopped to solicit entertainment.

In the gallery sat a fine, stalwart man, and a woman, who in size and figure matched him well. Some ruddy, fat children were playing on the steps. The man wore a full beard, which is very uncommon in these parts. I rode to a horse-block near the gallery, and asked if I could be accommodated for the night. "Oh, yes, you can stay here if you can get along without anything to eat; we don't have anything to eat but once a week." "You look as if it agreed with you, I reckon I'll try it for one night." "Alight, sir, alight. Why, you came from Texas, didn't you? Your rig looks like it," he said, as I dismounted. "Yes, I've just crossed Texas, all the way from the Rio Grande." "Have you though? Well, I'll be right glad to hear something of that country." He threw my saddle and bags across the rail of the gallery, and we walked together to the stable.

"I hear that there are a great many Germans in the western part of Texas," he said presently.

"There are a great many; west of the Guadalupe [River], more Germans than Americans born."

"Have they got many slaves?"

"No."

"Well, won't they break off and make a Free State down there, by and by?"

"I should think it not impossible that they might."

"I wish to God they would; I would like right well to go and settle there if it was free from slavery. You see Kansas and all the Free States are too far north for me; I was raised in Alabama, and I don't want to move into a colder climate; but I would like to go into a country where they had not got this curse of slavery."

He said this not knowing that I was a Northern man. Greatly surprised, I asked, "What are your objections to slavery, sir?"

"Objections! The first's here" (striking his breast); "I never could bring myself to like it. Well, sir, I know slavery is wrong, and God'll put an end to it. It's bound to come to an end, and when the end does come, there'll be woe in the land. And, instead of preparing for it, and trying to make it as light as possible, we are doing nothing but make it worse and worse. That's the way it appears to me, and I'd rather get out of these parts before it comes. Then I've another objection to it. I don't like to have slaves about me. Now, I tell a nigger to go and feed your horse; I never know if he's done it unless I go and see; and if he didn't know I would go and see, and would whip him if I found he hadn't fed him, would he feed him? He'd let him starve. I've got as good niggers as anybody, but I never can depend on them; they will lie, and they will steal, and take advantage of me in every way they dare. Of course they will, if they are slaves. But lying and stealing are not the worst of it. I've got a family of children, and I don't like to have such degraded beings round my house while they are growing up. I know what the consequences are to children, of growing up among slaves."

I here told him that I was a Northern man, and asked if he could safely utter such sentiments among the people of this district, who bore the reputation of being among the most extreme and fanatical devotees of slavery. "I've been told a hundred times I should be killed if I were not more prudent in expressing my opinions, but, when it comes to killing, I'm as good as the next man, and they know it. I never came the worst out of a fight yet since I was a boy. I never am afraid to speak what I think to anybody. I don't think I ever shall be."

"Are there many persons here who have as bad an opinion of slavery as you have?"

"I reckon you never saw a conscientious man who had been brought up among slaves who did not think of it pretty much as I do—did you?"

"Yes, I think I have, a good many."

"Ah, self-interest warps men's minds wonderfully, but I don't believe there are many who don't think so, sometimes—it's impossible, I know, that they don't."

Were there any others in this neighbourhood, I asked, who avowedly hated slavery? He replied that there were a good many mechanics [manual workers, craftsmen], all the mechanics he knew, who felt slavery to be a great curse to them, and who wanted to see it brought to an end in some way. The competition in which they were constantly made to feel themselves engaged with slave-labour was degrading to them, and they felt it to be so. He knew a poor, hard-working man who was lately offered the services of three negroes for six years each if he would let them learn his trade, but he refused the proposal with indignation, saying he would starve before he helped a slave to become a mechanic. There was a good deal of talk now among them about getting laws passed to prevent the owners of slaves from having them taught trades, and to prohibit slave-mechanics from being hired out. He could go out to-morrow, he supposed, and in the course of a day get two hundred signatures to a paper alleging that slavery was a curse to the people of Mississippi, and praying the Legislature to take measures to relieve them of it as soon as practicable. (The county contains three times as many slaves as whites.)

He considered a coercive government of the negroes by the whites, forcing them to labour systematically, and restraining them from a reckless destruction of life and property, at present to be necessary. Of course, he did not think it wrong to hold slaves, and the profits of their labour were not more than enough to pay a man for looking after them—not if he did his duty to them. What was wrong, was making slavery so much worse than was necessary. Negroes would improve very rapidly, if they were allowed, in any considerable measure, the ordinary incitements to improvement. He knew hosts of negroes who showed extraordinary talents, considering their opportunities: there were a great many in this part of the country who could read and write, and calculate mentally as well as the general run of white men who had been to schools. There were Colonel——'s negroes, some fifty of them; he did not suppose there were any fifty more contented people in the world; they were not driven hard, and work was stopped three times a day for meals; they had plenty to eat, and good clothes; and through the whole year they had from Friday night to Monday morning to do what they liked with themselves. Saturdays, the men generally worked in their patches (private gardens), and the women washed and mended clothes. Sundays, they nearly all went to a Sabbath School which the mistress taught, and to meeting, but they were not obliged to go; they could come and go as they pleased all Saturday and Sunday; they were not looked after at all. . . .

Beyond the excessive labour required of them on some plantations, he did not think slaves were often treated with unnecessary cruelty. It was necessary to use the lash occasionally. Slaves never really felt under any moral obligation to obey their masters. Faithful service was preached to them as a Christian duty, and they pretended to acknowledge it, but the fact was that they were obedient just far as they saw that they must be to avoid punishment; and punishment was necessary, now and then, to maintain their faith in their master's power. He had seventeen slaves, and he did not suppose that there had been a hundred strokes of the whip on his place for a year past.

He asked if there were many Americans in Texas who were opposed to slavery, and if they were free to express themselves. I said that the wealthy Americans there were all slaveholders themselves; that their influence all went to encourage the use of slave-labour, and render labour by whites disreputable. "But are there not a good many Northern men there?" he asked. The Northern men, I replied, were chiefly merchants or speculators, who had but one idea, which was to make money as fast as they could; and nearly all the little money there was in that country was in the hands of the largest slaveholders.

If that was the way of things there, he said, there could not be much chance of its becoming a Free State. I thought the chances were against it, but if the Germans continued to flock into the county, it would rapidly acquire all the characteristic features of a free-labour community, including an abundance and variety of skilled labour, a home market for a variety of crops, denser settlements, and more numerous social, educational, and commercial conveniences. There would soon be a large body of small proprietors, not so wealthy that the stimulus to personal and active industry would have been lost, but yet able to indulge in a good many luxuries, to found churches, schools, and railroads, and to attract thither tradesmen, mechanics, professional men, and artists. Moreover, the labourers who were not landholders would be intimately blended with them in all their interests; the two classes not living dissociated from each other, as was the case generally at the South, but engaged in a constant fulfilment of reciprocal obligations. I told him that if such a character of society could once be firmly and extensively established before the country was partitioned out into these little independent negro kingdoms, which had existed from the beginning in every other part of the South, I did not think any laws would be necessary to prevent slavery. It might be a slave State, but it would be a free people.

On coming from my room in the morning, my host met me with a hearty grasp of the hand. "I have slept very little with thinking of what you told me about western Texas. I think I shall have to go there. If we could get rid of slavery in this region, I believe we would soon be the most prosperous people in the world."

55. MOVING INTO ALABAMA HILL COUNTRY

Northern Alabama, June 15th. — I have to-day reached a more distinctly hilly country — somewhat rocky and rugged, but with inviting dells. The soil is sandy and less frequently fertile; cotton-fields are seen only at long intervals, the crops on the small proportion of cultivated land being chiefly corn and oats. I notice also that white men are more commonly at work in the fields than negroes, and this as well in the cultivation of cotton as of corn.

The larger number of the dwellings are rude log huts, of only one room, and that unwholesomely crowded. I saw in and about one of them, not more than fifteen feet square, five grown persons, and as many children. Occasionally, however, the monotony of these huts is agreeably varied by neat, white, frame houses. . . .

I passed the night at the second framed house that I saw during the day, stopping early in order to avail myself of its promise of comfort. It was attractively situated on a hill-top, with a peach orchard near it. The proprietor owned a dozen slaves, and "made cotton," he said, "with other crops." He had some of his neighbours at tea and at breakfast; sociable, kindly people, satisfied with themselves and their circumstances, which I judged from their conversation had been recently improving. One coming in, remarked that he had discharged a white labourer whom he had employed for some time past; the others congratulated him on being "shet" of him; all seemed to have noticed him as a bad, lazy man; he had often been seen lounging in the field, rapping the negroes with his hoe if they didn't work to suit him. "He was about the meanest white man I ever see," said a woman; "he was a heap meaner 'n niggers. I reckon niggers would come somewhere between white folks and such as he." "The first thing I tell a man," said another, "when I hire him, is, 'if there's any whippin' to be done on this place I want to do it myself.' If I saw a man rappin' my niggers with a hoe-handle, as I see him, durned if I wouldn't rap him—the lazy whelp."

One of the negroes complimented my horse. "Dar's a heap of genus in dat yar hoss's head!" The proprietor looked after the feeding himself.

These people were extremely kind; inquiring with the simplest good feeling about my domestic relations and the purpose of my journey. When I left, one of them walked a quarter of a mile to make sure that I went upon the right road. The charge for entertainment [food and lodging], though it was unusually good, was a quarter of a dollar less than I have paid before, which I mention . . . as an indication of the habits of the people, showing, as it may, either closer calculation, or that the district grows its own supplies, and can furnish food cheaper than those in which attention is more exclusively given to cotton.

56. HUNTING DOGS AND THEIR PREY

June 17th.—The country continues hilly, and is well populated by farmers, living in log huts, while every mile or two, on the more level and fertile land, there is a larger farm, with ten or twenty negroes at work. A few whites are usually working near them, in the same field, generally ploughing while the negroes hoe.

. . .

. . . I rode on through a valley, narrow and apparently fertile, but the crops indifferent. The general social characteristics were the same that I met with yesterday.

At night I stopped at a large house having an unusual number of negro cabins and stables about it. The proprietor, a hearty old farmer, boasted much of his pack of hounds, saying they had pulled down five deer before he had had a shot at them. He was much interested to hear about Texas, the Indians and the game. He reckoned there was "a heap of big varmint out thar."

His crop of cotton did not average two bales to the hand, and corn not twenty bushels to the acre. . . .

The farmer told me something about "nigger dogs"; they didn't use foxhounds, but bloodhounds—not pure, he thought, but a cross of the Spanish bloodhound with the common hounds, or curs. There were many men, he said, in the country below here, who made a business of nigger-hunting, and they had their horses trained, as well as the dogs, to go over any common fence, or if they couldn't leap it, to break it down. Dogs were trained, when pups, to follow a nigger—not allowed to catch one, however, unless they were quite young, so that they couldn't hurt him much, and they were always taught to hate a negro, never being permitted to see one except to be put in chase of him. . . . He had seen a pack of thirteen who would follow a trail two days and a half old, if rain had not fallen in the mean time. When it rained immediately after a negro got off, they had to scour the country where they supposed he might be till they scented him.

When hard pushed, a negro always took to a tree; sometimes, however, they would catch him in an open field. When this was the case the hunter called off the dogs as soon as he could, unless the negro fought—"that generally makes 'em mad (the hunters), and they'll let 'em tear him a spell. The owners don't mind having them kind o' niggers tore a good deal; runaways ain't much account no-how, and it makes the rest more afraid to run away, when they see how they are sarved." If they caught the runaway within two or three days, they got from $10 to $20; if it took a longer time, they were paid more than that; sometimes $200. They asked their own price; if an owner should think it exorbitant, he supposed, he said in reply to an inquiry, they'd turn the nigger loose, order him to make off, and tell his master to catch his own niggers.

57. VISIT WITH A TENNESSEE "SQUIRE"

To-day, I am passing through a valley of thin, sandy soil, thickly populated by poor farmers. Negroes are rare, but occasionally neat, new houses, with other improvements, show the increasing prosperity of the district. The majority of dwellings are small log cabins of one room, with another separate cabin for a kitchen; each house has a well, and a garden inclosed with palings. Cows, goats, mules and swine, fowls and doves are abundant. The people are more social than those of the lower country, falling readily into friendly conversation with a traveller. They are very ignorant; the agriculture is wretched and the work hard. I have seen three white women hoeing field crops to-day. A spinning-wheel is heard in every house, and frequently a loom is clanging in the gallery, always worked by women; every one wears homespun. The negroes have much more individual freedom than in the rich cotton country, and are not unfrequently heard singing or whistling at their work.

. . . At nightfall I entered a broader and more populous valley than I had seen before during the day, but for some time there were only small single room log cabins, at which I was loath to apply for lodging. . . .

Fortunately I did not have to go much further before I came to the best house I had seen during the day, a large, neat, white house, with negro shanties, and an open log cabin in the front yard. A stout, elderly fine-looking woman, in a cool white muslin dress, sat upon the gallery, fanning herself. Two little negroes had just brought a pail of fresh water, and she was drinking of it with a gourd, as I came to the gate. I asked if it would be convenient for her to accommodate me for the night, doubtingly, for I had learned to distrust the accommodations of the wealthy slaveholders.

"Oh yes, get down; fasten your horse there, and the niggers will take care of him when they come from their work. Come up here and take a seat."

I brought in my saddle-bags.

"Bring them in here, into the parlour," she said, "where they'll be safe."

The interior of the house was furnished with unusual comfort. "The parlour," however, had a bed in it. As we came out, she locked the door.

We had not sat long, talking about the weather (she was suffering much from the heat), when her husband came. He was very hot also, though dressed coolly enough in merely a pair of short-legged,

unbleached cotton trousers, and a shirt with the bosom spread open—
no shoes nor stockings. He took his seat before speaking to me, and
after telling his wife it was the hottest day he ever saw, squared his chair
toward me, threw it back so as to recline against a post, and said gruffly,
"Good evening, sir; you going to stay here to-night?"

I replied, and he looked at me a few moments without speaking. He
was, in fact, so hot that he spoke with difficulty. At length he got breath
and asked abruptly: "You a mechanic, sir, or a dentist, eh—or what?"

Supper was cooked by two young women, daughters of the master of
the house, assisted by the two little negro boys. The cabin in front of the
house was the kitchen, and when the bacon was dished up, one of the
boys struck an iron triangle at the door. "Come to supper," said the host,
and led the way to the kitchen, which was also the supper-room. . . .

A big lout of a youth who came from the field with the negroes,
looked in, but seeing me, retired. His father called, but his mother said,
"'twouldn't do no good—he was so bashful."

Speaking of the climate of the country, I was informed that a majority
of the folks went barefoot all winter, though they had snow much of the
time four or five inches deep, and the man said he didn't think most of
the men about here had more than one coat, and they never wore any in
winter except on holidays. "That was the healthiest way," he reckoned,
"just to toughen yourself and not wear no coat"; no matter how cold it
was, he didn't wear no coat. . . .

. . . When I went down stairs in the morning, having been wakened
early by flies, and the dawn of day through an open window, I saw the
master lying on his bed in the "parlour," still asleep in the clothes he
wore at supper. His wife was washing her face on the gallery, being
already dressed for the day; after using the family towel, she went into
the kitchen, but soon returned, smoking a pipe, to her chair in the
doorway.

Yet everything betokened an opulent and prosperous man—rich
land, extensive field crops, a number of negroes, and considerable herds
of cattle and horses. He also had capital invested in mines and railroads,
he told me. His elder son spoke of him as "the squire."

A negro woman assisted in preparing breakfast (she had probably
been employed in the field labour the night before), and both the young
ladies were at the table. The squire observed to me that he supposed
we could buy hands very cheap in New York. I said we could hire them
there at moderate wages. He asked if we couldn't buy as many as we
wanted, by sending to Ireland for them and paying their passage. He
had supposed we could buy them and hold them as slaves for a term

of years, by paying the freight on them. When I had corrected him, he said, a little hesitatingly, "You don't have no black slaves in New York?" "No, sir." "There's niggers there, ain't there, only they're all free?" "Yes, sir." "Well, how do they get along so?" "So far as I know, the most of them live pretty comfortably." (I have changed my standard of comfort lately, and am inclined to believe that the majority of the negroes at the North live more comfortably than the majority of whites at the South.) "I wouldn't like that," said the old lady. "I wouldn't like to live where niggers was free, they are bad enough when they are slaves: it's hard enough to get along with them here, they're so bad. I reckon that niggers are the meanest critters on earth; they are so mean and nasty" (she expressed disgust and indignation very strongly in her face). "If they was to think themselves equal to we, I don't think folks could abide it — they're such vile saucy things." A negro woman and two boys were in the room as she said this.

58. CAROLINA HIGHLANDERS' CRITIQUE OF SLAVERY

North Carolina, July 13th. — I rode late last night, there being no cabins for several miles in which I was willing to spend the night, until I came to one of larger size than usual, with a gallery on the side toward the road and a good stable opposite it. A man on the gallery was about to answer (as I judged from his countenance), "I reckon you can," to my inquiry if I could stay, when the cracked voice of a worryful woman screeched out from within, "We don't foller takin' in people."

"No, sir," said the man, "we don't foller it."

"How far shall I have to go?"

"There's another house a little better than three quarters of a mile further on."

To this house I proceeded — a cabin of one room and a loft, with a kitchen in a separate cabin. The owner said he never turned anybody away, and I was welcome. He did not say that he had no corn, until after supper, when I asked for it to feed my horse. The family were good-natured, intelligent people, but very ignorant. The man and his wife and the daughters slept below, the boy and I in the cock-loft. Supper and breakfast were eaten in the detached kitchen. Yet they were by no means poor people. The man told me that he had over a thousand acres of rich tillable land, besides a large extent mountain range, the most of which latter he had bought from time to time as he was able, to prevent the settlement of squatters near his valley-land. "There were people who would be bad neighbors, I knew," he said, "that would settle on most any kind of place, and everybody wants to keep such as far away from them as they can." (When I took my bridle off, I hung it up by the stable door; he took it down and said he'd hang it in a safer place. He'd never had anything stolen from here, and he didn't mean to have—it was just as well not to put temptation before people, and he took it into the house and put it under his bed.)

Besides this large tract of land here, he owned another tract of two hundred acres with a house upon it, rented for one-third the produce, and another smaller farm, similarly rented; he also owned a grist mill, which he rented to a miller for half the tolls. He told me that he had thought a good deal formerly of moving to new countries, but he had been doing pretty well and had stayed here now so long, he didn't much think he should ever budge. He reckoned he'd got enough to make him a living for the rest of his life, and he didn't know any use a man had for more'n that.

I did not see a single book in the house, nor do I think that any of the family could read. He said that many people here were talking about Iowa and Indiana; "was Iowa (Hiaway) beyond the Texies?" I opened my map to show him where it was, but he said he "wasn't scollar'd enough" to understand it, and I could not induce him to look at it. I asked him if the people here preferred Iowa and Indiana to Missouri at all because they were Free States. "I reckon," he replied, "they don't have no allusion to that. Slavery is a great cuss, though, I think, the greatest there is in these United States. There ain't no account of slaves up here in the west, but down in the east part of this State about Fayetteville there's as many as there is in South Carolina. That's the reason the West and the East don't agree in this State; people out here hates the Eastern people."

"Why is that?"

"Why, you see they vote on the slave basis, and there's some of them nigger counties where there ain't more'n four or five hundred white folks, that has just as much power in the Legislature as any of our mountain counties where there'll be some thousand voters."

He made further remarks against slavery and against slaveholders. When I told him that I entirely agreed with him, and said further, that poor white people were usually far better off in the Free than in the Slave States, he seemed a little surprised and said, "New York ain't a Free State, is it?"

. . .

. . . I stopped last night at the pleasantest house I have yet seen in the highlands; a framed house, painted white, with a log kitchen attached. The owner was a man of superior standing. I judged from the public documents and law books on his table, that he had either been in the Legislature of the State [of North Carolina], or that he was a justice of the peace. There were also a good many other books and newspapers, chiefly of a religious character. He used, however, some singularly uncouth phrases common here. He had a store, and carried on farming and stock raising. After a conversation about his agriculture, I remarked that there were but few slaves in this part of the country. He wished that there were fewer. They were not profitable property here, I presumed. They were not, he said, except to raise for sale; but there were a good many people here who would not have them if they were profitable, and yet who were abundantly able to buy them. They were horrid things, he thought; he would not take one to keep it if it should be given to him. 'Twould be a great deal better for the country, he believed, if there was not a slave in it. He supposed it would not be right to take them away from those who had acquired property in them, without any remuneration, but he wished they could all be sent out of the country—sent to Liberia. That was what ought to be done with them. I said it was evident that where there were no slaves, other things being equal, there was greater prosperity than where slavery supplied the labour. He didn't care so much for that, he said; there was a greater objection to slavery than that, in his mind. He was afraid that there was many a man who had gone to the bad world, who wouldn't have gone there if he hadn't had any slaves. He had been down in the nigger counties a good deal, and he had seen how it worked on the white people. It made the rich people, who owned the niggers, passionate and proud, and ugly, and it made the poor people mean. "People that own niggers are always mad with them about something; half their time is spent in swearing and yelling at them."

"I see you have 'Uncle Tom's Cabin' here," said I; "have you I read it?"

"Oh, yes."

"And what do you think of it?"

"Think of it? I think well of it."

"Do most of the people here in the mountains think as you do about slavery?"

"Well, there's some thinks one way and some another, but there's hardly any one here that don't think slavery's a curse to our country, or who wouldn't be glad to get rid of it."

I asked what the people about here thought of the Nebraska Bill.[1] He couldn't say what the majority thought. Would people moving from here to Nebraska now, be likely to vote for the admission of slavery there? He thought not; "most people would much rather live in a Free State." He told me that he knew personally several persons who had gone to California, and taken slaves with them, who had not been able to bring them back. There were one or two cases where the negroes had been induced to return, and these instances had been made much of in the papers, as evidence that the slaves were contented.

"That's a great lie," he said; "they are not content, and nine-tenths of 'em would do 'most anything to be free. It's only now and then that slaves, who are treated unusual kind, and made a great deal of, will choose to remain in slavery if freedom is put in their way." He knew one man (giving his name) who tried to bring two slaves back from California,[2] and had got started with them, when some white people suspecting it, went on board the ship and told him it was against the law to hold negroes as slaves in California, and his negroes shouldn't go back with him unless they were willing to. Then they went to the slaves and told them they need not return if they preferred to stay, and the slaves said they had wanted very much to go back to North Carolina, yet they would rather remain in California, if they could be free, and so they took them ashore. He had heard the slave owner himself relating this, and cursing the men who interfered. He had told him that they did no more than Christians were obliged to do.

I overtook upon the road, to-day, three young men of the poorest class. Speaking of the price of land and the profit of farming, one of them said, believing me to be a Southerner—

"We are all poor folks here; don't hardly make enough to keep us in liquor. Anybody can raise as much corn and hogs on the mountains as he'll want to live on, but there ain't no rich people here. Nobody's got any black ones—only three or four; no one's got fifty or a hundred, like as they have down in the East." "It would be better," interrupted another, somewhat fiercely, "there warn't any at all; that's my mind about it; they're no business here; they ought to be in their own country

---

[1] A reference to what soon would become the Kansas-Nebraska Act, legislation passed by Congress later in 1854. In the name of "popular sovereignty," it stipulated that these two territories could determine their status as slave or free based on a vote by current residents.

[2] California entered the Union as a free state as part of the Compromise of 1850, despite the fact that many southern gold prospectors had come into the new state with slave property.

and take care of themselves, that's what I believe, and I don't care who hears it." But let the reader not be deceived by these expressions; they indicate simply the weakness and cowardice of the class represented by these men. It is not slavery they detest; it is simply the negro competition, and the monopoly of the opportunities to make money by negro owners, which they feel and but dimly comprehend.

59. WITH SLAVES AND WITHOUT: TWO MOUNTAIN FARMS COMPARED

North-eastern Tennessee,——.—Night before last I spent at the residence of a man who had six slaves; last night, at the home of a farmer without slaves. Both houses were of the best class common in this region; two-story framed buildings, large, and with many beds, to accommodate drovers and waggoners, who, at some seasons, fill the houses which are known to be prepared with stabling, corn, and beds for them. The slaveholder was much the wealthier of the two, and his house originally was the finer, but he lived in much less comfort than the other. His house was in great need of repair, and was much disordered; it was dirty, and the bed given me to sleep in was disgusting. He and his wife made the signs of pious people, but were very morose or sadly silent, when not scolding and re-ordering their servants. Their son, a boy of twelve, was alternately crying and bullying his mother all the evening till bed-time, because his father had refused to give him something that he wanted. He slept in the same room with me, but did not come to bed until after I had once been asleep, and then he brought another boy to sleep with him. He left the candle burning on the floor, and when, in five minutes after he had got into bed, a girl came after it, he cursed her with a shocking volubility of filthy blackguardism [abuse], demanding why she had not come sooner. She replied gently and entreatingly, "I didn't think you'd have more'n got into bed yet, master John." The boys were talking and whispering obscenity till I fell asleep again. The white women of the house were very negligent and sluttish in their attire; the food at the table badly cooked, and badly served by negroes.

The house of the farmer without slaves, though not in good repair, was much neater, and everything within was well-ordered and unusually comfortable. The women and girls were clean and neatly dressed; every one was cheerful and kind. There was no servant. The table was abundantly supplied with the most wholesome food—I might almost say the first wholesome food—I have had set before me since I was at the hotel at Natchez; loaf bread for the first time; chickens, stewed instead of fried; potatoes without fat; two sorts of simple preserved fruit, and whortleberry and blackberry tarts. (The first time I have had any of these articles at a private house since I was in Western Texas.) All the work, both within and without the house, was carried on regularly and easily, and it was well done, because done by parties interested in the result, not by servants interested only to escape reproof or punishment.

Doubtless two extreme cases were thus brought together, but similar, if less striking, contrasts are found the general rule, according to my experience. It is a common saying with the drovers and waggoners of this country, that if you wish to be well taken care of, you must not stop at houses where they have slaves.

The man of the last described house was intelligent and an ardent Methodist. The room in which I slept was papered with the "Christian Advocate and Journal," the Methodist paper of New York. At the slaveholder's house, my bedroom was partially papered with "Lottery Schemes."

The free labouring farmer remarked, that, although there were few slaves in this part of the country, he had often said to his wife that he would rather be living where there were none. He thought slavery wrong in itself, and deplorable in its effects upon the white people. Of all the Methodists whom he knew in North-eastern Tennessee and South-western Virginia, he believed that fully three fourths would be glad to join the Methodist Church North, if it were "convenient." They generally thought slavery wrong, and believed it the duty of the church to favour measures to bring it to an end. He was not an Abolitionist, he said; he didn't think slaves could be set free at once, but they ought to be sent back to their own country, and while they were here they ought to be educated.

He had perceived that great injustice was done by the people both of the North and South, towards each other. At the South, people were very apt to believe that the Northerners were wanting not only to deprive them of their property, but also to incite the slaves to barbarity and murder. At the North, people thought that the negroes were all very inhumanely treated. That was not the case, at least hereabouts, it wasn't. If I would go with him to a camp meeting here, or to one of the common Sunday meetings, I would see that the negroes were generally better dressed than the whites. He believed that they were always well fed, and they were not punished severely. They did not work hard, not nearly as hard as many of the white folks; they were fat and cheerful. I said that I had perceived this, and it was so generally, to a great degree, throughout the country; yet I was sure that on the large plantations it was necessary to treat the slaves with great severity. He "expected" it was so, for he had heard people say, who had been on the great rice and cotton plantations in South Carolina, that the negroes were treated very hard, and he knew there was a man down here on the railroad, a contractor, who had some sixty hands which he had hired in Old Virginny ("that's what we call Eastern Virginia here"), and everybody who saw them at work, said he drove them till they could hardly stand, and did not give them half what they ought to have to eat. He was opposed to the Nebraska Bill, he said, and to any further extension of slavery, on any pretext; the North would not do its Christian duty if it allowed slavery to be extended; he wished that it could be abolished in Tennessee.

He thought that many of the people who went hence to Kansas would vote to exclude slavery, but he wasn't sure that they would do it generally, because they would consider themselves Southerners, and would not like to go against other Southerners. A large part of the emigration from this part of the country went to Indiana, Illinois, and Iowa; those States being preferred to Missouri, because they were Free States. There were fewer slaves hereabouts now, than there were when he was a boy. The people all thought slavery wrong, except, he supposed, some slaveholders who, because they had property in slaves, would try to make out to themselves that it was right. He knew one rich man who had owned a great many slaves. He thought slavery was wrong, and he had a family of boys growing up, and he knew they wouldn't be good for anything as long as he brought them up with slaves; so he had told his slaves that if they wanted to be free, he would free them, send them to Liberia, and give them a hundred dollars to start with, and they had all accepted the offer. He himself never owned a slave, and never would own one for his own benefit, if it were given to him, "first, because it was wrong; and secondly, because he didn't think they ever did a man much good."

I noticed that the neighbours of this man on each side owned slaves; and that their houses and establishments were much poorer than his.

A Cotton Kingdom Chronology
(1822–1861)

1822   *April 26* Frederick Law Olmsted born in Hartford, Connecticut.

1843   Olmsted embarks as a sailor on a yearlong voyage to China; in 1851 he recounts the experience in a journal article, "A Voice from the Sea."

1846–
1848   Mexican War; U.S. victory results in the acquisition of the Mexican provinces of California, New Mexico, and Texas.

1848   Olmsted's father purchases a farm for him on Staten Island, New York.

1850   Olmsted travels through Europe with his brother, John Hull, and friend Charles Loring Brace.

        Compromise of 1850 seeks to resolve the dispute over the spread of slavery in the territories; key elements include the admission of California as a free state and the passage of the Fugitive Slave Act.

1852   Olmsted's first book, *Walks and Talks of an American Farmer in England*, published.

        Harriet Beecher Stowe's *Uncle Tom's Cabin* published.

        Olmsted hired by Henry J. Raymond, editor of the *New York Daily Times*, to tour the American South as a roving correspondent.

1852–
1853   *December–April* Olmsted's first trip to the South.

1853–
1854   *February–February* Olmsted's forty-eight dispatches, called "The South," published on an almost weekly basis in the *New York Daily Times*.

        November–May Olmsted's second trip through the South, accompanied by his brother.

155

1854 *March–June* Olmsted's fifteen dispatches, called "A Tour in the Southwest," published in the *New York Daily Times*.

May–July Olmsted's third and final trip through the South, following the return home of John Hull.

Kansas-Nebraska Act divides the region into two territories and stipulates that the issue of slavery in each will be decided on the basis of popular sovereignty.

Formation of the Republican party, committed to a "free-soil" agenda.

1855 Olmsted becomes a partner in the New York publishing firm Dix & Edwards; he travels throughout Europe on its behalf for much of 1856.

1856 Olmsted's *A Journey in the Seaboard Slave States* published.

"Bleeding Kansas" undermines the policy of popular sovereignty.

1857 Olmsted's *A Journey through Texas* published.

Olmsted becomes the superintendent of Central Park in New York City.

1860 *August* Olmsted's *A Journey in the Back Country* published.

November–December Lincoln's election as president triggers the secession crisis, with South Carolina leaving the Union on December 20.

1861 Six more southern states secede by February 1. After the Confederate attack on Fort Sumter (April 12) ignites the U.S. Civil War, four more states secede by June 1.

February–June On the suggestion of Olmsted's British publisher, Olmsted works with coeditor Daniel Goodloe to condense his three volumes of southern travel writing into one, *The Cotton Kingdom*; he composes a new introductory chapter called "The Present Crisis."

October *The Cotton Kingdom* is published in England; a month later, an American edition is issued.

Questions for Consideration

1. What developments in the 1850s made Olmsted's writings on slavery and the South particularly timely? In what ways did his commentary on those topics differ from that of other writers at the time?

2. How did Olmsted's attitude toward the South change between his early reports on the region in 1853 and 1854 and the culmination of his southern travel writing, *The Cotton Kingdom*, in 1861? What factors explain his shift in thinking?

3. Olmsted spent considerable time in southern cities during his trips. Based on his commentary, what role did the urban South play in the region's economy and the place of slavery within that economy?

4. Where, in the course of his southern travels, did Olmsted encounter the worst treatment of slaves? Where did he encounter the best? Explain his reactions to both.

5. Judging from Olmsted's account, what was the impact of Harriet Beecher Stowe's *Uncle Tom's Cabin* on southerners?

6. Olmsted documented a wide range of uses of slave labor. What was the most unusual or unconventional use of slaves he witnessed? What most surprised him in that regard?

7. What do we learn from Olmsted about overseers and other taskmasters employed on southern plantations? What sort of judgments did Olmsted render as to their effectiveness and their treatment of those who fell under their charge?

8. What evidence do we find in *The Cotton Kingdom* regarding Olmsted's attitudes toward race? What struck you as his most racist comments in the book? Why?

9. What conclusions can one draw about the status of southern women, both white and black, from Olmsted's commentary on those he encountered or observed?

10. Which of Olmsted's several encounters with African Americans, slave or free, do you find most revealing? Why?

11. Olmsted spent time on farms and plantations that produced tobacco, cotton, rice, and sugar. What differences in the use of slaves in these operations are most apparent based on his descriptions?

12. How would you assess Olmsted's characterization of poor whites during his journeys? Which encounter with nonslaveholding whites do you find most revealing? Why?

13. Where did Olmsted encounter the most antislavery attitudes among southern whites? What were the rationales for their opposition? Note specific instances of statements he heard and relates in his narrative.

14. At what points does Olmsted make his case regarding southern backwardness most effectively? What do you find to be his most striking examples of the cultural, educational, or economic inferiority of the South compared with the North?

15. Olmsted used a variety of modes of transportation throughout his southern travels. What do they and his descriptions of them suggest about southern life and economic development in the mid-1850s? What do you find to be the most interesting encounters he had with fellow travelers? Why?

16. What were Olmsted's most effective arguments to British readers as to why they should cast their lot with the Union instead of the Confederacy?

Selected Bibliography

OLMSTED

Hall, Lee. *Olmsted's America: An "Unpractical" Man and His Vision of Civilization.* Boston: Little, Brown, 1995.

Martin, Justin. *Genius of Place: The Life of Frederick Law Olmsted.* Cambridge, Mass.: Da Capo Press, 2011.

Mitchell, Broadus. *Frederick Law Olmsted: A Critic of the Old South.* Baltimore: Russell & Russell, 1924.

Olmsted, Frederick Law. *The Papers of Frederick Law Olmsted.* Vol. 1: *The Formative Years, 1822–1852.* Edited by Charles Capen McLaughlin and Charles E. Beveridge. Baltimore: Johns Hopkins University Press, 1977; and Vol. 2, *Slavery and the South, 1852–1857.* Edited by Charles Capen McLaughlin and Charles E. Beveridge. Baltimore: Johns Hopkins University Press, 1981.

Olmsted, Frederick Law, Jr., and Theodora Kimball. *Frederick Law Olmsted: Landscape Architect, 1822–1903.* New York: G. P. Putnam's Sons, 1922.

Roper, Laura Wood. *FLO: A Biography of Frederick Law Olmsted.* Baltimore: Johns Hopkins University Press, 1973.

Rybczynski, Witold. *A Clearing in the Distance: Frederick Law Olmsted and America in the Nineteenth Century.* New York: Scribner's, 1999.

Schlesinger, Arthur M., ed. *The Cotton Kingdom: A Traveller's Observations on Cotton & Slavery in the American Slave States,* by Frederick Law Olmsted. New York: Alfred A. Knopf, 1953.

Stevenson, Elizabeth. *Park Maker: A Life of Frederick Law Olmsted.* New York: Macmillan, 1977.

Todd, John Emerson. *Frederick Law Olmsted.* Boston: Twayne, 1982.

OTHER FIRSTHAND ACCOUNTS OF THE SOUTH

Berwanger, Eugene H. *As They Saw Slavery.* Minneapolis: Winston Press, 1973.

Cox, John D. *Traveling South: Travel Narratives and the Construction of American Identity.* Athens: University of Georgia Press, 2005.

Hoffman, Charles, and Tess Hoffman. *North by South: The Two Lives of Richard James Arnold.* Athens: University of Georgia Press, 1988.

Inscoe, John C. *Race, War, and Remembrance in the Appalachian South.* Lexington: University Press of Kentucky, 2008.

Lockard, Joe. *Watching Slavery: Witness Texts and Travel Reports.* New York: Peter Lang, 2008.

Parrish, T. Michael. *Richard Taylor: Soldier Prince of Dixie.* Chapel Hill: University of North Carolina Press, 1992.

Wilson, Edmund. *Patriotic Gore: Studies in the Literature of the American Civil War.* New York: Oxford University Press, 1962.

SLAVERY AND THE SECTIONAL CRISIS

Ashworth, John. *The Republic in Crisis, 1848–1861.* New York: Cambridge University Press, 2012.

Berlin, Ira. *Generations of Captivity: A History of African-American Slaves.* Cambridge, Mass.: Harvard University Press, 2003.

Cooper, William J. *The South and the Politics of Slavery, 1828–1856.* Baton Rouge: LSU Press, 1978.

Crawford, Martin. *The Anglo-American Crisis of the Mid-Nineteenth Century: The Times and America, 1850–1862.* Athens: University of Georgia Press, 1987.

Davis, David Brion. *Inhuman Bondage: The Rise and Fall of Slavery in the New World.* New York: Oxford University Press, 2006.

Fogel, Robert W. *Without Consent or Contract: The Rise and Fall of American Slavery.* New York: W. W. Norton, 1989.

Ford, Lacy K. *Deliver Us from Evil: The Slavery Question in the Old South.* New York: Oxford University Press, 2009.

Foreman, Amanda. *A World on Fire: An Epic History of Two Nations Divided.* New York: Random House, 2011.

Fredrickson, George M. *The Inner Civil War: Northern Intellectuals and the Crisis of the Union.* New York: Harper & Row, 1965.

Freehling, William W. *The Road to Disunion.* 2 vols. New York: Oxford University Press, 1990, 2007.

Genovese, Eugene D. *The Political Economy of Slavery: Studies in the Economy and Society of the Slave South.* New York: Vintage, 1967.

———. *Roll, Jordan, Roll: The World the Slaves Made.* New York: Vintage, 1974.

Gossett, Thomas F. *Uncle Tom's Cabin and American Culture.* Dallas: Southern Methodist University Press, 1985.

Johnson, Walter. *River of Dark Dreams: Slavery and Empire in the Cotton Kingdom.* Cambridge, Mass.: Harvard University Press, 2013.

Jones, Howard. *Blue & Gray Diplomacy: A History of Union and Confederate Foreign Relations.* Chapel Hill: University of North Carolina Press, 2010.

———. *Union in Peril: The Crisis over British Intervention in the Civil War.* Chapel Hill: University of North Carolina Press, 1992.

Morgan, Kenneth, ed. *Slavery in America: A Reader and Guide.* Athens: University of Georgia Press, 2005.

Potter, David M. *The Impending Crisis, 1848–1861.* New York: Harper Torchbooks, 1976.

Reynolds, David S. *Mightier Than the Sword: Uncle Tom's Cabin and the Battle for America.* New York: W. W. Norton, 2011.

Rothman, Adam. *Slave Country: American Expansion and the Origins of the Deep South.* Cambridge, Mass.: Harvard University Press, 2005.

Walther, Eric. *The Shattering of the Union: America in the 1850s.* Wilmington, Del.: Scholarly Resources, 2004.

Index